THE CHARACTER OF CREATION

*Exploring the relationship between Biblical
creation and modern scientific discoveries*

DAVID M. DORIA

The Character of Creation

© 2012 David M. Doria

All rights reserved. No part of this publication may be reproduced, stored in a retrieval system, or transmitted in any form or by any means—for example, electronic, photocopy, recording—without the prior written permission of the publisher. The only exception is brief quotations in printed reviews.

Unless otherwise indicated, Scripture taken from the *New King James Version*. Copyright © 1979, 1980, 1982 by Thomas Nelson, Inc. Used by permission. All rights reserved.

Scripture quotations marked HCSB are taken from the *Holman Christian Standard Bible*(R), Copyright ©1999, 2002, 2003 by Holman Bible Publishers. Used by permission. *Holman Christian standard Bible(R)*, and *HCSB(R)* are federally registered trademarks of Holman Bible Publishers.

Scripture quotations marked KJV are taken from *The Holy Bible King James Version*, public domain.

Cover based on original painting and photo by Mary E. Doria.

Published by Inspired Science Publications,
Lakewood, CA., USA.

ISBN-10: 0615604692
EAN-13: 9780615604695

TABLE OF CONTENTS

Introduction	*v*
1. *The Ordinances of the Heavens*	*1*
2. *Design*	*7*
3. *God and Gravity*	*15*
4. *Windows of Vision*	*19*
5. *The Delicate Balance*	*25*
6. *The Obedient Creation*	*29*
7. *Precept Upon Precept*	*33*
8. *The Unique Creation*	*41*
9. *A Higher View*	*47*
10. *The Skillful Creation*	*55*
11. *The Praising Creation*	*59*
12. *The Complexity Chasm*	*63*
13. *The Aging Creation*	*69*
14. *The Conservative Creation*	*75*
15. *The Dust of Creation*	*83*
16. *The Rational Universe*	*91*
17. *The Causal Creation*	*103*
18. *Home Sweet Home*	*111*
19. *Purposes of Creation*	*119*
20. *The Uncreative Creation*	*125*
21. *The Stretched-Out Universe*	*129*
22. *The Temperature of Creation*	*133*

23. The Constants of Creation	139
24. Reflections of Splendor	145
25. The Waters of Creation	149
26. The Paradoxical Universe	157
27. The Magnificent Creation	163
28. His Mighty Torrential Rains	167
29. Entropy and the Arrow of Time	175
30. The Sustained Creation	179
31. Line Upon Line	183
32. Where to Look	189
33. The Big Creation	193
34. The Extent of the Universe	199
35. The Created Creation	203
36. The Heavens for Height	209
37. The Separate Creation	215
38. The Goodness of Creation	219
39. The Severity of Creation	225
40. The Power of Creation	231
41. The Creation Inspires	235
42. The Secretive Creation	239
43. The Mathematical Language of the Universe	247
44. To Everything a Purpose	255
45. The Invisible Creation	261
Notes	269

INTRODUCTION

*"The heavens declare the glory of God;
And the firmament shows His handiwork." (Psalm 19:1)*

"You established the earth, and it abides." (Psalm 119:90)

"Beware lest anyone cheat you through philosophy and empty deceit, according to the tradition of men, according to the basic principles of the world, and not according to Christ." (Colossians 2:8)

The fields of science and theology have often been fields of battle. This is particularly so in the arena of creation, where the camps have at times been entrenched. Perhaps, though, some amount of progress towards a mutual understanding of views and perspectives can be had by an examination of what has been learned in science, and how particular areas of scientific knowledge relate to theology, Scripture and to creation. I hold to a high view of science, that it is a tremendously important enterprise carried out by sincere and dedicated people who have a passion for their work. Historically, a number of prominent scientists have also been men who had faith in the God of the Bible.

Among this number are Galileo, Kepler, Newton, Boyle, Faraday, Maxwell, and Lord Kelvin, to name just a few, and the list could be expanded and extended to present-day working scientists. Clearly these founders of modern science saw no fundamental conflict between their faith-based worldviews and their scientific endeavors.

Since our topic revolves (perhaps elliptically) around the dual foci of both theology and science, I have tried in this book's various chapters to relate different aspects of Biblical revelation and theology to their discovery and outworking in different areas of mainstream science. There has been a remarkable set of developments in astronomy and cosmology that have occurred in the past hundred years or so, wherein areas of creation-related theology and science are both relevant. These areas of theology and science interact and intersect, and each makes specific statements about the physical world. One implication of taking Scripture as a source of truth is that Biblical revelation is not limited to morals and beliefs as some would like to confine it. Scripture really does speak about the created realm, and in doing so touches on areas that also fall within the domain of interest to science. A review of the progress in astronomy, cosmology and other scientific disciplines shows a remarkable unity between Biblical truth and scientific discovery---so much so that it is truly amazing. My hope is that in reading these chapters, scientists and those with an interest in science may discover a new perspective on Scripture and faith, and that fellow Christians may find that science is not necessarily hostile to their deeply held beliefs.

Introduction

One definition of character is a thing's "main or essential nature" (1). If designed for a purpose, the object's character will reflect such purpose, and also may allow inferences as to the nature of its designer. For example, one might discern how knowledgeable, wise, well intentioned, clever, innovative, economical, thoughtful, resourceful, or good the designer is. This book touches with a broad brush on a number of possible such inferences. For instance, the aspect of the creation regarding physical law points to the Creator's faithfulness and eternal power. There is a vast and grand scale to this universe, signifying an even more extraordinary and grand Creator. The creation's highly organized original state is discussed with respect to both the forward direction of time and the inadequacy of chance-based explanations for existence (both the entire universe's and ours), and points to the fact that the world was formed by an all-wise God. The limited duration of observable creation, that it had a definite beginning, is now acknowledged by mainstream cosmology. This is also a Biblical perspective. The creation has traits of both goodness and severity, as does the Creator (Romans 11:22). The act of science itself is driven by the character of creation. Without a fundamental rationality to the laws of nature, the practice of science as we comprehend it would not be possible. In fact, the universe appears designed, from the smallest to the broadest scales, for those who wish to be challenged, to observe and to understand its physical order. Remarkably, the creation seems to have a language, that of essential, deep and even beautiful mathematics, woven into its very fiber. There is also a glory associated with the natural creation that is above our ability to comprehend, inspiring artists throughout the generations and causing us to look beyond the cosmos for a Helper and True Author of salvation. Each of these themes, and others, contributes to the character of creation.

The book's Scriptural perspective is Christian. The Biblical book of Proverbs states: "The Lord by wisdom founded the earth; By understanding He established the heavens; By His knowledge the depths were broken up; And clouds drop down the dew" (Proverbs 3:19-20). Psalm 107:8 implores "Oh that men would praise the Lord for his goodness, and for his wonderful works to the children of men" (KJV). Thus, it is profitable to apply study to the Earth and the heavens so that we may in some small way come to appreciate the glorious wisdom and understanding that was necessary for their creation. One of the founders of modern science, Johann Kepler, wrote of a psalm "I implore my reader not to forget the divine goodness conferred on mankind, and which the psalmist urges him especially to consider"(2). In his research and writings, Kepler seems to have been struck by the grandeur and extent of the Creator's providence in the creation.

As regards the relationship between science and theology, orthodox Christians hold that God both created the heavens and Earth and also fully inspired the Biblical Scriptures. It follows that any correct understanding of both science and Scripture cannot be contradictory since they both proceed from a single Perfect and True Author. Thus diligent study of the Biblical Scriptures and attention to scientific facts are both profitable, and consequently the modern presumptive mind-set of absolute naturalism[*] is viewed as too restrictive. My approach in discussing creation and related scientific topics has been to proceed from the basic premise, as revealed by the book of Genesis, that there is a Creator God. Further, there are precepts and claims of Holy Scripture which we take to be true based on Scriptural inerrancy. Jesus Himself endorsed the absolute veracity of Scripture in John 10:35 when He said "the Scripture cannot be broken." In thus regarding Biblical revelation as the legitimate and true form of knowledge available to mankind, we proceed from an unchanging and unchangeable foundational support regarding the nature of our world, and seek to include scientific discoveries that may inform our understanding. I thereby direct my comments, with a sincere hope and desire that such will inspire a sense of discovery of the reality of Him whose "kingdom rules over all" (Psalm 103:19), with increased acknowledgment of His glory through observations of His "handiwork," and in that discovery and acknowledgment, stimulate an attitude of faith toward His Son, Jesus Christ our Lord and Savior.

David M. Doria
Lakewood, CA

---

[*] Naturalism in its absolute form is a doctrine that presupposes that supernatural causes are nonexistent.

1

THE ORDINANCES OF THE HEAVENS

"Do you know the ordinances of the heavens?
Can you set their dominion over the earth?" (Job 38:33)

"Forever, O Lord, Your word is settled in heaven.
Your faithfulness endures to all generations;
You established the earth, and it abides.
They continue this day according to Your ordinances,
For all are Your servants." (Psalm 119:89-91)

"Thus says the Lord, Who gives the sun for a light by day,
The ordinances of the moon and the stars for a light by
night..." (Jeremiah 31:35)

The Character of Creation

"'If those ordinances depart from before Me, says the Lord, then the seed of Israel shall also cease from being a nation before Me forever.'" (Jeremiah 31:36)

"This most beautiful system of the sun, planets, and comets, could only proceed from the counsel and dominion of an intelligent and powerful Being." Isaac Newton (1)

Men have had a fascination with the heavenly realm since ancient times. What is it? Where is it? Are its elements different from those on the Earth? How did the heavenly bodies get there? What holds them up? Of what do they consist? How distant are they? For ages these and similar questions have attracted the attentions of virtually all cultures. About four hundred years ago, after millenia of speculation and rather unscientific concepts, the initial setting forth of what we now think of as the basic laws of physics caused quite a stir in the thinking of Western civilization. One historian cites the approximately 150 year period between 1543, the year of publication of Copernicus's theory, and the end of the 17th century as a critical time period in this new era (2). It was during this time that reason in science became increasingly independent of historical philosophies. Also, new and improved instruments of observation were invented and applied in the use of scientific inquiry, and observations began to be coupled to notions of evidence for support of hypotheses about the natural world. The change in attitude and understanding that these innovations brought about was so great that we still refer to this extended set of events as the Scientific Revolution. Perhaps the most celebrated of the changes in viewpoint was the notion of a broad governance of motion by orderly and fairly simple physical laws, which Isaac Newton set forth in his universal law of gravity and three laws of motion. Over time other laws and constants of nature have been discovered so that accepted and received physics today is that the entire universe is governed by what we call "laws" of physics. But where did these laws come from? What is their nature? Do they change or can they be changed? Does something or Someone govern the laws themselves?

The books of Jeremiah, Job and Psalms (see above) stated well over two millenia ago that there are ordinances or statutes whereby the stars, moon and heavens are governed by God's providence. Therefore, Christian faith and doctrine are entirely consistent with the assertion and discovery of physical law as characterized by the decrees of God. Thus one of the most fundamental characteristics of the physical creation is that there exist created physical laws, and that these laws apparently apply to all physical existence, as supported by Psalm 119:89-91 and Job 38:33. These laws are, physically speaking, pervasive, all encompassing, and apparently ever in force, while also subject to the Creator's authority. This is consistent with the character of these laws that God declared many years ago by His prophets.

According to Strong's dictionary (3), the word for ordinances in Jeremiah 31:36 also connotes enactments or commandments. The ordinances or statutes of the heavens, as elements of creation, are not self-existent based on any proven theory of physics. That is, they require an explanation just as any other physical phenomena, and must not be regarded as some sort of primordial "gods" that are eternal on their own and responsible for the universe. Atheistic arguments typically make presumptions that build on the characteristics of physical law but do not actually explain the origin of the laws or of their properties; thus such arguments fall flat as explanations for the universe. The Scripture clearly indicates that the one True and Living God created the heavens and the Earth, and the ordinances are spoken of as "of" the moon and the stars in Jeremiah 31:35 and Job 38:33, and not above or beyond or before the celestial creation. The physical laws of the universe evidently are therefore a part of the creation, perhaps one of its most fundamental parts. As such they are a consequence of God's creative act. Their universal applicability is demonstrative of the God of creation's universal hand of governance, and not of the independence of nature from God.

The Copernican and Newtonian revolutions forever changed our view of the place of the Earth in the universe, and of the universe itself with respect to God. For some, these changes also led to a changed worldview of the relationship of man to nature. Nature took on more of the perceived role of governor and displaced the view of the Lord as Creator, Upholder and Nurturer of nature. However, this so-called modern view, which is still prevalent in today's science and philosophy, is actually a deviation from the views of a number of the key influential founders of modern science. While differing in Biblical doctrines, many of these early scientists were sincere believers in a Creator God according to the Judeo-Christian tradition. For example Kepler, Copernicus, Galileo, Newton, Boyle and Faraday were all sincere and highly committed believers in God. Historically, it appears that it was never the intention of these early great discoverers of what we regard as natural laws to undermine or replace faith in God. In their day, science and the scientific establishment were not opposed to the notion of a Creator God who also designed and sustained the universe. Indeed, historian J. H. Brooke points out that their faith seems to have been one of the factors that led the early scientific researchers to undertake the investigative search for physical laws (4). Based on theologically informed philosophical and scientific views of an orderly and rational creation that was consistent with the revelation of God's character in the Bible, the expectation of these great early scientists was consequently the discovery of a rational and orderly creation. For example, Kepler's researches seem to have been directly inspired by his faith in a rational God (5). With this conception of nature, Kepler discovered three laws of planetary motion that helped set the stage for the discoveries of Newton. This philosophic scientific foundation is quite the opposite of the popular view of science that we are inundated with today, which for the most part (at least officially) is generally either agnostic or atheistic. Indeed, the relevance of faith to the founders of modern science strikes the popular ear as somewhat odd, but would not do so except for the extreme bias that we see today against revealed Scriptural truth in the world of science and its various official and extended popular media outlets.

The study of physics is concerned with the discovery of natural physical laws and their properties and applications. The Bible does not set out the specifics of these laws, but it did inform us that they were there long before science arrived at the concept of physical law. Scriptural truth in this area preceded the developments of modern science, and is in no way contradicted by those later developments. In fact, the developments of modern science have confirmed a number of the scientific statements that are in the Biblical Scriptures, and have never refuted a single one.

2

DESIGN

"So God created man in His own image; in the image of God He created him; male and female He created them." (Genesis 1:27)

"Then the rib which the Lord God had taken from man He made into a woman..." (Genesis 2:22)

"Before the mountains were brought forth, Or ever You had formed the earth and the world..." (Psalm 90:2)

"Hast thou not heard long ago, how I have done it; and of ancient times, that I have formed it?"
(Isaiah 37:26 (KJV))

"Know that the Lord, He is God; it is He who has made us, and not we ourselves..." (Psalm 100:3)

For scientists and non-scientists alike, the impression of design is often strongly felt in the grandeur, fascination, intricacy and beauty of nature. That there is a manifest imprint of order placed into the creation itself is obvious even to young children. Careful investigation into the way things truly are actually supports these impressions. This is especially true in our modern world, in which knowledge of physics, cosmology, biology and biochemistry is compounding yearly. Such knowledge, contrary to the line fed to many university students, points clearly in the direction of design. A famous quote by noted astronomer Fred Hoyle remarks "A common sense interpretation of the facts suggests that a super intellect has monkeyed with physics, as well as chemistry and biology, and that there are no blind forces worth speaking about in nature" (1). A philosophy of science that defies this "common sense" view is certainly not mandated by the empirical facts of nature. Unfortunately, but not unexpectedly, this is nonetheless the direction that the scientific establishment has selected. Lest they succumb to to the force of the evidence, eminent scientists must exhort their colleagues that the fantastic biochemical structures that abound in nature were not actually designed (2). No less than a definition of what is allowed within science is in dispute. This would seem, primarily, because of an artificial philosophical commitment to absolute naturalism* as a prerequisite to science (3). Within such a system, only physical causes and explanations are acceptable. However, as pointed out by Poe and Davis, this is actually a philosophical position and not a scientific one (4). It cannot be proved by science.

Such an absolute restriction to physical-material causes within science is too limiting according to modern design theorists (5). There is nothing more "scientific" about naturalism than there is about design, and both can potentially be involved in the causes for the way things are. The proper challenge for the scientist is to find the best explanation based on the evidence, without excluding a feasible class of explanations a priori. Many if not most of the inventors of modern science held to a faith in God. In general these men were not offended by the possibility of God's hand in nature. To propose the possibility of design in nature allows for other direct or indirect causes such as the effects of the laws of physics or chance. But not all entities in existence can reasonably be attributed to these two causes. For example, nobody would say that Shakespeare's sonnets were written by a horde of monkeys randomly

---

* Absolute naturalism entails a view that only physical causes are allowable as potential explanations in science. Such a view excludes God's hand from His creation.

striking keyboards. According to one mathematician, the universe would undergo heat death before such an unlikely occurrence (6). Instead, it is agreed that someone (the "who was Shakespeare?" question is another matter) actually wrote them (i.e. "designed" the received pattern of the letters and words). This is uncontroversial; the odds of the "monkey" explanation are just too far-fetched for any rational person to accept. However, when faced with the same or greater overwhelming odds against the spontaneous appearance of life in the world, and the existence of a world and universe that is capable of supporting life, the random-chance option is all that is allowed by modern science. What is being presented in our modern media and educational institutions is a revisionist view of science that presumes but cannot prove the sufficiency of materialist causes (7).

There is extremely strong evidence that design of a very precise nature has pervaded the creation from its inception. By analyzing the initial conditions of the universe, Roger Penrose has estimated that the odds against the initial state of the universe are less than one part in $10^{10^{123}}$ (8)*. These chances are so tiny as to virtually eliminate all possibility of non-design, and to invoke chance in this area is just as absurd as the "monkey" explanation of the sonnets. Very specific physical evidence pointing to design of the universe is discussed by astronomer Hugh Ross (9). He reviews the precise

---

* Note that there are much less than $10^{10^{123}}$ protons and neutrons in the entire universe.

"settings" for a number of the physical constants of the universe that are remarkably arranged to support life. Fine-tuning that far exceeds any of man's best machinery is exhibited by the cosmic mass density and the space energy density, which are within the "just right" values to within one part in 10 to the sixtieth and one part in ten to the 120th, respectively. Chance cannot account for these evidences, and there is no law of physics that explains them.

Regarding the observation of physically constituted life on our planet, Dr. John R. Baumgardner goes through an interesting argument regarding the chances of a cell "just happening" (i.e. the chances that chemical evolution explains the first living cell) (10). Given all the time available since the beginning of the universe billions of years ago, he calculates the likelihood that chance could have produced a simplest possible living cell at any place in the universe. Taking the total possible molecules in the universe as a starting point for chemical evolution (a very generous allowance on the side of chemical evolution), billions of years of reactions (again, quite generous), and a large (relative to what would actually happen) number of inter-atomic reactions per second per atom, he arrives at an upper bound of the possible number of unique molecules that could have ever existed since the universe began. Then, assuming a minimum number of proteins for the simplest possible cell of about 1000, and that for each of these one half of the proteins would need to be specified precisely, and also that by luck 999 of the proteins already exist, he calculates the probability of that last protein coming into existence by chance in the universe, since the universe began. Baumgardner's calculation shows that even considering all the time and opportunities physically possible, the overall chance that even a single successful assembly of that final 1000th protein will occur is virtually nil. And remember, we didn't count against these odds that there had to be 999 useful proteins already there (other estimates are lower in terms of the number of required proteins but do not change the overall force of this argument) and that they were in very close proximity (on the molecular scale of distances), and that they were not degraded by competing chemical reactions which are also known to be present in real-world conditions. Further, we ignored the fact that all biologically active amino acids (the "dice" in this random experiment) are left-handed, but that the right- and left-handed amino acids both behave the same way in chemical reactions, and so there has to be some yet-unexplained method of separating them out. Also, we left out the fact that there would need to simultaneously exist some kind of reproduction mechanism (proteins do not self-replicate on their own). A chemical such as RNA or DNA or some other type of reproductive information-transmitting chemical mechanism would have to "come together" also at the same time as the proteins, and that this is just as unlikely as the above described protein synthesis. When these factors are combined, the likelihood of a "chance" occurrence of life is eliminated within all reasonable bounds. Darwin, of course, did not know any of this, and it seems that much of the science world has more faith in his ignorance than appreciation for the statistical impossibility of chance chemical evolution, imposed by a genuine scientific appreciation of the complexity of even the simplest possible life.

The mass media and scientific establishment would still have us choose the random-chance explanation regardless of any appeal to the odds, or a necessity-driven explanation without substantive proof. Design theorists, on the contrary, prefer that a genuine search for the truth should not be so artificially constrained, and that a truly modern view of science ought to demand that it include the possibility of design as an explanation for some observations, including creation itself and life. William Dembski's explanatory filter comes into play here (11). The process of examination he describes allows the possibilities of natural law, chance or design for any effect. Preference is given strongly to law and chance over design to the level of extreme improbability (12). According to Dembski, this process of review for the contingencies of law and chance, and finally specification with complexity, lead to a reliable method of classifying observations in science as designed or not. Those in search of naturalistic explanations for the first cell must either find some undiscovered natural law or laws leading to the self-organization of life, or refute the statistical arguments that show that chance cannot explain the cell. However, there are no known natural laws to account for the spontaneous creation of even one living cell, and the chances of such an occurrence have been shown to be absurdly small even if the random process were to be given all the time since the beginning the universe, and all the material in the universe. Thus, we are compelled to conclude wonderful DESIGN!

3

God and Gravity

"Then Joshua spoke to the Lord in the day when the Lord delivered up the
Amorites before the children of Israel, and he said in the sight of Israel:
'Sun, stand still over Gibeon; And Moon, in the Valley of Aijalon.'
So the sun stood still, And the moon stopped,
Till the people had their revenge upon their enemies.
Is this not written in the Book of Jasher? So the sun stood still in the midst of heaven, and did not hasten to go down for about a whole day. And there has been no day like that, before it or after it, that

the Lord heeded the voice of a man; for the Lord fought for Israel." (Joshua 10:12-14)

"He hangs the earth on nothing..." (Job 26:7)

*"...and in Him all things consist."
(Colossians 1:17, speaking of Jesus Christ)*

Perhaps the best-known physical law is that of gravity. The effects of its pull are constantly visible to us and felt by us. Spilled coffee falls to the ground rather than floating around in the air or rising up to the ceiling. Kites fall to the ground if not held up by enough wind. The moon faithfully stays in orbit around the Earth, the Earth and planets around the sun, and the sun about the center of the Milky Way galaxy, all testifying to gravity's pervasive effects. Historically, the actual determination of the physical characteristics of the law of gravity required the use of astronomical observations due to the relative weakness of its force (it is by far the weakest of the four known fundamental forces of nature). Gravity's effects at long distances as a result of interactions between massive bodies are measurable, and were quantifiable even hundreds of years ago. Building on Tycho Brahe's data, Johann Kepler described three mathematical properties of the orbits of the planets about the sun. Newton proceeded to generalize the attractive force of gravity, which he formalized as being proportional to the inverse of the square of the distances between two bodies, and proportional to the product of their masses. Newton also proposed that "We must ...universally allow that all bodies whatsoever are endowed with a principle of mutual gravitation" (1). This was an insight that directly contradicted the remaining influences of ancient Greek Aristotelian physics, which held to the notion that the behavior and essence of the heavenly bodies was in some fundamental way different from the behavior of matter on Earth.

The publication of the universal law of gravity and Newton's three laws of motion revolutionized the thinking of Western man. Whereas some thought to view the so-called "mechanical universe" as separate from God, and by extension without need of God, this was apparently never in the mind of Newton. To the contrary, Newton did not hold to a purely mechanical view of the created natural order (2). Neither apparently did he adhere even to a deistic view of God as relates to the workings of the planets, as he apparently believed that their orbits might become unstable if not corrected every so often by God. Newton's religious beliefs, which were quite serious[*], seem to have been to him entirely compatible with his science. He himself wrote: "When I wrote my treatise about our System I had an eye upon such Principles as might work with considering men for the belief of a Deity &

---

[*] Newton wrote extensively on his interpretations of Biblical topics.

nothing can rejoice me more than to find it useful for that purpose" (3).

Our uniquely Western view of a universe that behaves according to prescribed laws is compatible with a creation that was ordained by the Creator whose character is revealed in the Judeo-Christian Bible. The providence of God is in no way threatened by the laws of nature; what was challenged by the scientific revolution was the previous medieval view of the relationship between God and nature. Examination of what the Bible actually *says* is of the highest importance in this regard. When this is done, we find no actual errors in Scripture, or provable contradictions between known facts of science and Scriptural revelation. We must remember that the God of the Bible is the God of the whole universe and rules over its laws. When Christ said "Are not two sparrows sold for a copper coin? And not one of them falls to the ground apart from your Father's will" (Matthew 10:29), He clearly was teaching us to trust God and not live life in fear of its circumstances, but He also used an analogy that included God's providence acting within and through the laws of nature, including gravity's pull on a small bird. It appears plain that the parable is meant to be applied to our lives and lived out in the real world, where God is still in control beyond what we can see, think, or even imagine.

4

WINDOWS OF VISION

"For now we see in a mirror, dimly, but then face to face."
(1 Corinthians 13:12)

"When I consider the heavens, the work of Your fingers,
the moon and the stars, which You have ordained,
What is man that You are mindful of him,
And the son of man that You visit him?" (Psalm 8:3-4)

"Then He brought him outside and said, 'Look now toward
the heaven, and count the stars if you are able to number
them.' And He said to him, 'So shall your descendants be.'

And he believed in the Lord, and He accounted it to him for righteousness." (Genesis 15:5- 6)

"Where there is no vision, the people perish..."
(Proverbs 29:18 (KJV))

"I believe in Christianity as I believe that the sun has risen. Not only because I see it, but because I see everything by it."
C.S. Lewis (1)

My son has a book about how things work, in which is a picture of a radio telescope (2). At first blush the idea of taking astronomical pictures with radio waves would seem to be a pretty far-fetched idea, and yet today this type of instrument is very real, and in fact is a standard instrument that is used to peruse the heavens in search of its secrets. Other telescopes detect X-rays and gamma rays from the farthest reaches of the universe. Indeed, these are just a few examples of the phenomenal diversity of methods of observation that have been afforded us by the Creator. Each involves the measurement of some aspect of electromagnetic (EM) radiation. Some of the properties of EM radiation are more familiar than others to our everyday experience. One of the most common, perhaps without our being explicitly aware of it, is the spectral wavelength diversity of different material reflectances, which our eye-brain system exploits to give us color vision. Thus the impression of the hue of a pink rose is due to the spectral distribution of reflected sunlight off of the petals, transmitted through air, detected by the spectrally tuned receptors in our eyes, and interpreted by our brains and minds. The complexity of the physics and psycho-physics is staggering, resulting in an appreciation of the beauty of the flower's color, texture and delicate shape.

It was none other than Isaac Newton who invented the first reflective telescope, which uses a mirror instead of a lens to focus light. It is interesting to note that the Scripture reference from 1 Corinthians 13:12 mentions the imperfections of our current observations of spiritual reality, using an analogy to observation in a physical mirror. In the case of a reflecting or refracting telescope, the mirror and lens diameters are actually one of the fundamental limits to the effective resolution and sensitivity, which is why astronomers love big telescopes.

Our natural perceptions of electromagnetic radiation are extremely wonderful and are an amazing gift from God. However, our eyes are designed to only capture a small sliver of the actual electromagnetic spectrum, and even with magnifying instruments our observations are imperfect. The visible light that we perceive is that portion of the EM spectrum between approximately .4 and .7 microns (millionths of a meter) wavelength. The EM spectrum extends orders of magnitude in wavelength on both sides of this window, and in the last few hundred years the Lord has granted mankind the knowledge to design instruments that can measure these extended portions of the spectrum. The remarkable quality of the creation that allows us to look through these "windows" to observe its physical nature may be regarded as a fundamental aspect of its character. By exploiting these "windows of vision," astronomers are now able to see details of the universe that previous generations could not have imagined.

One of the windows to the universe is our atmosphere, which turns out to be quite extraordinary. As described by Gonzalez and Richards, the Earth's atmosphere has a number of very special properties including high transmittance of light at the wavelengths that are emitted in large proportion by the sun, and which are used by plants for photosynthesis and detected by many animals and by human beings to allow vision (3). Because of the high degree of transparency of visible light through our atmosphere, we have been able to measure properties of the solar system and stars using precise optical measurements. For example, helium was discovered in spectra of the sun before it was discovered on Earth.

It is a remarkable fact that, as Gonzalez and Richards point out, the portion of the spectrum including near ultraviolet, visible and near infrared, that which is in the neighborhood of human visible response, comprises a mere one part in ten to the 25th power of the total natural electromagnetic emissions of the universe (4). On the side of "very small" windows of vision, we now have electron microscopes that focus on extremely tiny particles for the purpose of observing the inward structure of cells to reveal their biochemical and microbiological structure. Far from being the relatively simple blobby structures that were thought to comprise cells in the late nineteenth and early twentieth centuries, we now have pictures of exquisite microstructures such as membranes and mitochondria comprising a large number of subparts of living cells. In the field of diagnostic medicine, X-rays with much smaller wavelengths than visible light are so routinely used that it is a rare person in the civilized world who reaches their 30th birthday without having had at least one. On the larger wavelength side of the EM spectrum with respect to the visible window, radio communication (including both radio and television) is one of the definers of the modern age, and radio telescopes allow amazing pictures of the universe at these longer wavelengths, revealing aspects of celestial objects that are otherwise unmeasurable.

Gonzalez and Richards draw out a theme of the universe that discusses the truly wonderful confluence of the requirements for both life and observation (5). It appears that our ability to "see" the creation is a gift, and our solar system's special place in the galaxy is one of the only places that such observation coupled with habitation would be possible. It is as if God wanted us to observe His creation and give Him glory with understanding, as He says in Romans 1:20 "For since the creation of the world His invisible attributes are clearly seen, being understood by the things that are made." As we peek through these windows, we are only taking little glimpses into what God has already prepared and is allowing us to observe.

5

THE DELICATE BALANCE

*"For He looks to the ends of the earth,
And sees under the whole heavens,
To establish a weight for the wind,
And apportion the waters by measure." (Job 28:24- 25)*

*"For He draws up drops of water,
Which distill as rain from the mist,
Which the clouds drop down
And pour abundantly on man." (Job 36:27- 28)*

The Character of Creation

*"To Him who by wisdom made the heavens,
For His mercy endures forever..." (Psalm 136:5)*

Scientists have discovered remarkable balances between the relative magnitudes of the constants of nature. It turns out that for quite a few cases the proportionate values of the constants are observed to be very finely arranged. In physics the well-known "fine-structure constant," or alpha, has a value of 1/137.03599976. Alpha relates by a simple ratio the charge of the electron, Planck's constant and the speed of light, three fundamental constants of nature. It has been observed by historians of science that alpha appears widely in quantum electrodynamics (1), which affects just about everything. Alpha's value is precisely balanced, at just the proper mix of electromagnetism, quantum mechanics and light. As pointed out by Barrow and Webb, if this value were only 4 percent larger there would be no carbon produced in stars, and organic chemistry (which is the chemistry inside us) would not exist (2); and if alpha were greater than .1, there would be no stars at all.

In another example in which movement of a physical constant either way would be disastrous, philosopher Robin Collins compares the force of gravity to the observed range of force magnitudes in nature (3). The assumption is that since this range of strengths actually exists in nature, this is a reasonable interval over which to draw comparisons. It is thus not arbitrary in terms of its magnitudes, and the relationships between the force magnitudes naturally gives rise to the method of analysis. He points out that if an imaginary "scale" were to be extended across the entire universe, with the numerical strength of the force of gravity on one side of this imaginary ruler and the strength of the strong nuclear force on the other side, that if the force of gravity were to be moved proportionately by only one inch, there would be no life as we know it in the universe. Even the slightest increase or decrease in the force magnitude of gravity relative to the other force magnitudes would change the universe too much for any type of physical life to have existed. In our human experience, balancing of parameters to this scale of precision is virtually impossible. And yet, it is a fact that these balances exist in nature and are, for the most part, taken for granted by us.

In multi-instrument orchestral music, it is the relationship of the individual notes for each instrument to those of the others that gives rise to the magnificence of a musical creation. To dismiss the astounding relationships between the constants that exist in the world of physics is something like saying that Beethoven's Fifth Symphony was a chance result of some guinea pigs with dirty feet running around on a piece of music notation paper one evening. On the contrary, it is much more straightforward to believe that the laws of the universe, entailing the structure and strengths of the forces and constants of nature, were orchestrated by God as an intrinsic property of nature, pointing to the infinite wisdom of the Creator.

6

THE OBEDIENT CREATION

*"...My right hand has stretched out the heavens;
When I call to them, they stand up together."
(Isaiah 48:13)*

"But as one was cutting down a tree, the iron ax head fell into the water; and he cried out and said, 'Alas, master! For it was borrowed.' So the man of God said, 'Where did it fall?' And he showed him the place. So he cut off a stick, and threw it in there; and he made the iron float. Therefore he said, 'Pick it up for yourself.' So he reached out his hand and took it." (2 Kings 6:5-7)

"Then He arose and rebuked the wind, and said to the sea, 'Peace, be still!' And the wind ceased and there was a great calm. But he said to them, 'Why are you so fearful? How is it that you have no faith?' And they feared exceedingly, and said to one another, 'Who can this be, that even the wind and the sea obey Him!'" (Mark 4:39-41)

"Now in the fourth watch of the night Jesus went to them, walking on the sea." (Matthew 14:25)

We see time and again in Scripture that the creation is instantly subject to God's word. This is an attribute of creation that truly is beyond science. Thus our view of nature is changed from that of a closed system sufficient unto itself, to a created order that is subject to God to suit His purposes. Some of God's purposes may be impervious to our understanding, while others are revealed in Scripture. God Himself is beyond science and is not limited whatsoever by its rules. For that reason, some in so-called science would try to exclude the miraculous interventional power of God from any possible activity in the physical realm. This was seen in the 17th and 18th centuries by deistic-type philosophers as some sort of advantage for God, as if He were demonstrating additional perfection by not interfering, or by designing a creation that never could be interfered with by Himself. This trend continues in an even more vehement form in our own day, as advocates of naturalistic philosophy and the new atheism try to convert the populace into their way of thinking. However, neither deism nor pure naturalism are the doctrines of Scripture. The creation is not in rebellion against God, nor is it indifferent to His rule. On the other hand, mankind rebelled against God in the garden, and unredeemed man is still not willingly subject to God's will.

It is interesting to consider how many of the miracles of Jesus convey His mastery over the laws of nature. Jesus's first public miracle, the changing of water into wine at the marriage of Cana, may seem innocuous enough, perhaps almost like a magic trick, until one considers what really transpired. Christ, without fanfare or any difficulty whatsoever, changed the elemental components of water to those of wine. This is not a feat that any chemist of today or any day could ever do, for it involves changing the constituents of matter. The words of the Bible treat this miracle as a significant event, indicating that in performing this act Jesus "manifested forth His glory" (John 2:11 (KJV)). In today's scientific view we can observe that to accomplish this miracle required absolute supremacy by Christ over the very laws of nuclear physics! It appears that the Master of creation did it virtually effortlessly. This miracle was an unmistakable demonstration of Jesus's ability to dominate the essential elements of this world, and it is in His demonstration of superiority over the natural laws themselves that the Scripture gives us one of the compelling proofs of Jesus Christ's divinity. It is as the Author of these laws that He can change and overrule them by command. Jesus Christ is referred to as the "Word" in John's gospel chapter 1, which informs us that "the Word was God" (John 1:1), and "the Word became flesh" (John 1:14). Speaking of Christ, John 1:3 says that "All things were made through Him, and without Him nothing was made that was made." Jesus demonstrated miraculous dominion over the laws of nature, turning water to wine, walking on water, commanding the wind and sea to be calm and even conquering death!

The creation, as a consistent element of its character, remains to this day subject to its Creator. The apostle Paul gives us an interesting exhortation regarding submission: "I beseech you therefore, brethren, by the mercies of God, that you present your bodies a living sacrifice, holy, acceptable to God, which is your reasonable service" (Romans 12:1). Submission to Christ is regarded by the apostle as the only "reasonable" life for the believer in Christ. In this we can take an example from the creation itself in voluntary obedience to God's Word.

7

PRECEPT UPON PRECEPT

"The Lord by wisdom founded the earth;
By understanding He established the heavens;
By His knowledge the depths were broken up,
And clouds drop down the dew." *(Proverbs 3:19-20)*

"His understanding is unsearchable." *(Isaiah 40:28)*

"Through wisdom a house is built,
And by understanding it is established;
By knowledge the rooms are filled
With all precious and pleasant riches." *(Proverbs 24:3-4)*

"Whom will he teach knowledge?
And whom will he make to understand the message?
Those just weaned from milk?...
For precept must be upon precept,
Precept upon precept,
Line upon line, line upon line,
Here a little, there a little." (Isaiah 28:9-10)

It has been remarked that it is impossible for the hummingbird to fly, except that it does. This diminutive vertebrate is the only bird that can hover or fly backwards. Amazingly, some can flap their wings at twice the frame rate of a standard video camera (1). The design of the hummingbird for flight is a marvel that remains a challenge for us to understand, even with our knowledge of modern aerodynamics. How actually does the bird stay aloft? For years scientists thought that its flight mechanics were much more similar to insects than to birds; however, a recent study with ultrafast photography has shown that approximately seventy-five percent of the hummingbird's lift comes from the downstroke and about twenty-five percent from the upstroke, whereas insects get about half from the upstroke and half from the downstroke, and other birds derive all their lift from the downstroke (2). So, the hummingbird flight mechanics would seem to be in between that of birds and insects.

The "precept upon precept" concept of learning about nature is well illustrated by the hummingbird example, and countless other examples could be made of man's ability to gain understanding by careful observation of the world. There are different levels of understanding as well. At one level we might say that we have an explanation of the flight of the hummingbird in terms of the basic laws of physics. We know from Newton that for every action there is an equal and opposite reaction. A hummingbird flying along is exerting force on the air surrounding its wings, which in turn is exerting an equal amount of force in the exactly opposite direction. This accords with the beating of the hummingbird's wings, and hence powered flight is enabled and understood according to a precept that is one of the basic principles of physics. While correct, this explanation is incomplete; it says nothing about the details of the hummingbird's wing articulation, motion, feathers, respiration, balance, energy use, fine control, etc. Hence, the study results discussed in the previous paragraph provide an improved (but still far from perfect) explanation of the hummingbird's apparently implausible ability. As the finer details of motion are brought into the explanation and observations are carefully used to establish a theory, the model of hummingbird flight is both improved and deepened. At present our analysis still remains incomplete, and yet we consider it to be fully rational based on our undergirding confidence that the laws of physics provide an "explanation" for flight even if the experts don't yet have it all worked out. This account illustrates a common everyday type of rationality that does not insist on an understanding of each detail of creation, and that remains stable due to a faith in the character of rationality and natural law that pervades the world we live in. The nature of creation motivates a confident expectation that research can yield ever deeper understanding in science and technology. The reasoning and learning embodied by the "precept upon precept" principle is one of the keys to the development of modern science and the scientific method, involving both progressive reasoning and gained understanding.

A familiar example from the world of physics of the precept-upon-precept principle is that of the development of the modern theory of atomic structure, which proceeded through the early Rutherford and Bohr models to the more sophisticated atomic model that we have today. Rutherford observed the alpha particle-scattering properties of atoms and, based on the measured scattering cross sections, theorized that most of the mass and positive charge of the atom was concentrated in a very small volume. These observations were quite a surprise to him, as he commented it was "as if you had fired a 15-inch shell at a piece of tissue paper and it came back and hit you" (3). His proposed model of the atom was not a quantum model, however. Later, Bohr's model was the first to apply quantum ideas to atomic electron orbitals, thereby explaining why only certain frequencies of radiation could be emitted or absorbed by given atoms and also giving a quantum justification for why electron orbitals do not decay (4). Bohr's set of rules involving orbitals gave tremendous insight into the relationships between quantum behavior and atomic structure, even if his simplistic notion of circular electron orbitals needed to be abandoned as the theory developed into its modern form which treats orbitals with probability-like functions. Another example of precept-upon-precept development is the physical understanding of the nature of light. Newton believed that light was embodied in particles, thus explaining why it traveled in straight paths. Thomas Young in the early 1800s countered with convincing experimental evidence, based on interference effects, that illustrated light's wavelike nature. One problem with the wave theory of light was that it could not explain the detailed observations of the photoelectric effect, in which electrons are produced in certain metals when light of a certain frequency or higher is impinged on their surface. If the frequency of the light were lower than a minimum threshold then no electrons were produced, no matter how intense the light. In 1905 Einstein explained this behavior by employing a quantized model of light in which the energy is proportional to the frequency, thereby lending support to the particle view of light. The modern physical view of light includes what is known as the wave-particle duality, where both aspects of light are considered to be part of its physical nature[*], manifesting different properties depending on how an experiment is set up, and adhering to wave function descriptions that "collapse" in certain cases.

---

[*] A photon or elementary package of electromagnetic radiation has both particle and wave properties, with the photon energy equal to Planck's constant times the frequency of the wave.

Not all the kinks in the known laws of nature have been ironed out. Penrose points out that in the current theory of quantum mechanics the transition from quantum to classical behavior is difficult to pin down, and he regards the current theory of quantum mechanics as needing some revisions despite its successes (5). Another example is in the field of string theory where researchers are attempting, among other things, to unify general relativity with quantum mechanics (these two highly successful theories don't currently agree in theoretical regimes corresponding to an initial time period of the universe where they were both operating on the same scale).

Man's progressive understanding of the universe has not removed God from the picture of the world. Those of us who are believers in Christ should not be the least bit surprised by this. The Lord of the Bible tells us that "He has made the earth by His power; He has established the world by His wisdom, and stretched out the heaven by His understanding" (Jeremiah 51:15).

Speaking of the progress of cosmological science, Robert Jastrow laments of the possible theological implications by remarking that developments have led to "a band of theologians who have been sitting there for centuries" (6). A robust faith in the Creator God, at its most basic level as it relates the world and the universe, supports the initiatives of exploration, discovery and progressive understanding. This manner of belief is consistent with a historical Christian faith that has nurtured many of the founders of modern science and civilization. From these our society has been bequeathed with a heritage that encourages diligent search and the application of man's creativity to intellectual enterprises such as science and theology, all the while trusting in God for his giftings and graces for true understanding and wisdom.

8

THE UNIQUE CREATION

"This is the history of the heavens and the earth when they were created, in the day that the Lord God made the earth and the heavens, before any plant of the field was in the earth and before any herb of the field had grown." (Genesis 2:4-5)

"By the word of the Lord the heavens were made, and all the host of them by the breath of his mouth." (Psalm 33:6)

"For he spoke, and it was done; He commanded, and it stood fast." (Psalm 33:9)

The Character of Creation

"So God created man in His own image; in the image of God He created him; male and female He created them."
(Genesis 1:27)

"And now the Lord says, Who formed me from the womb to be His Servant,
To bring Jacob back to Him..." (Isaiah 49:5)

The first law of thermodynamics, absorbed by every high-school chemistry student, dictates that matter-energy can neither be created nor destroyed. The chemical and nuclear processes that occur in nature simply transform matter and energy into different forms, but are not actually "creative" in the sense of bringing something into existence from absolutely nothing. Nor can these same processes or reactions dispose of matter-energy into nothingness. The famous Einsteinian equation $E=mc^2$ sets out the equivalence relationship of matter and energy in mathematical form, and is entirely consistent with the first law of thermodynamics in that matter and energy are interchangeable, but says nothing about their creation. And yet here we are, along with a tremendously big universe that has all the evidences, based on our astronomical observations and measurements, of having had an actual beginning in terms of time, space, matter and energy. People who trust in nature as creator must somehow get around this formidable thermodynamic principle that has been known since the nineteenth century.

Bible-believing Christians assert that nature is the result of a unique creative act by God. The book of Isaiah tells us: "My hand made all these things, and so they all came into being. [This is] the Lord's declaration" (Isaiah 66:2 (HCSB)). Thus we know, based on God's revelation, that nature did not create itself. According to Geisler, the doctrine of creation by Almighty God is an important tenet of Judeo-Christian Scripture (1). The creative activity demonstrated by God is not to be attributed to the elements of nature itself; to do so is idolatry. Nor is nature a co-creator or an active agent of creation. Scripture never attributes creative ability to the natural elements, and it is interesting to note that this absence is entirely consistent with the first law of thermodynamics. In this aspect of its description of the physical universe the Biblical Scripture is, as always, one hundred percent accurate.

There is actually no direct comparison between the creative act of God and the activities of man at the physical level. We as humans deal with things that exist, and we change or modify them in a number of different ways, whereas it is God who has actually created them to begin with. However, mankind has been gifted with certain creative capacities in the realms of human activity. The potential of these gifts is denoted with undeniable examples such as Bach and Handel in music, da Vinci in art, Newton and Einstein in physics, Edison in invention, Gilbert and Sullivan in musical plays, and the list goes on and on. There are examples of Biblical gifts of artistry and excellence. The prophet

Daniel, along with his companions, was given "wisdom and skill" by God in all the matters of learning even in the culture in which they were captives (Daniel 1:17). Daniel's giftings of an "excellent spirit, knowledge, understanding, interpreting dreams, solving riddles, and explaining enigmas" were acknowledged as coming from the Spirit of God (Daniel 5:12-14). The book of Psalms also speaks of inspired godly worshipers: "Both the singers and the players on instruments say, 'All my springs are in you'" (Psalm 87:7). Indeed, for all of us the expression of our gifts is something that is truly one of life's fulfilling activities. We as Christians ought to seek to express our individual creative capacities, bestowed on us by the Creator, to the glory of our Creator and Savior Jesus Christ.

Some have tried to impose naturalistic causes for creativity, placing their hope and faith in such fields as genetics, neuroscience, biochemistry, biophysics, computer science and engineering. While much has been learned, as discussed by Dembski, actual human cognitive capability has never been explained or simulated in these fields (2). Christians would expect such explanations to be forever lacking. We know that we have souls that transcend the physical, and thus by definition our dual physical and spiritual nature as human beings can never be reduced to mere chemistry and physics, no matter how complex. Those who persist in a materialist-reductionist-only research plan in cognitive science are like those described by the apostle Paul as "always learning and never able to come to the knowledge of the truth" (2 Timothy. 3:7).

A most important aspect of the current age of creation is the fact that God still wants to do a creative work of salvation in each person. We find in Genesis that God spoke the creation into existence. The phrase "Then God said" is used multiple times in Genesis chapter 1. In the gospels, the incarnate Word of God (Jesus Christ) was revealed to the world, and we were given the gospel (good news) as the "power of God to salvation for everyone who believes" (Romans 1:16). This power is made available for transformation and re-creation of lives by the power of God through faith in Christ. Christians are "born again" of the Spirit when they are cleansed of their sins by Jesus Christ. Paul declares this wonderful truth in 2 Corinthians 5:17: "Therefore, if anyone is in Christ, he is a new creation..."

9

A Higher View

"You have prepared the light and the sun.
You have set all the borders of the earth;
You have made summer and winter." (Psalm 74:16-17)

"For thus says the Lord, Who created the heavens,
Who is God, Who formed the earth and made it,
Who has established it,
Who did not create it in vain,
Who formed it to be inhabited..." (Isaiah 45:18)

The Character of Creation

"The heaven, even the heavens, are the Lord's;
But the earth He has given to the children of men."
(Psalm 115:16)

In the second century after Christ, the Greek astronomer Ptolemy set the course for 1400 years of astronomical thought with his Earth-centered system of astronomy. The Ptolemaic system employed an intricate formulation of circular motions called epicycles for each of the planets in order to explain their observed heavenly traversals with respect to the Earth. The philosophical and theological attraction to the Earth-centered model was pervasive during the period of the Middle Ages prior to Copernicus, even to the point of gaining theological status. Much of this theology was rooted in earlier Greek philosophy with its esteem of the importance of the circle in geometry (1). In the 16th century the new Copernican heliocentric theory challenged the entrenched astronomical concepts of the Middle Ages, and placed the "lantern of the universe," as Copernicus referred to the sun, at the center of the universe (2). Thus began a complete upheaval in astronomy and in science itself. The Copernican idea was a scientific model that seemed to conform more to a notion of scientific elegance than the competing complicated and arbitrary Ptolemaic models. In that certain theological implications were to follow the heliocentric scientific model, there began a meaningful dialogue between the claims of religion and those of science, a dialogue which in some aspects continues to the present day.

The new Copernican system was not anti-Christian although some portrayed it as such; in actuality it refuted ancient Greek astronomical and philosophical models that were promoted erroneously within the church and also within universities at that time (3). The new model took some time to get things right also. The old concept of circular planetary orbits prevailed, even in the Copernican model, until Kepler published his three laws of planetary motion that showed that the orbits of the planets were elliptical and not circular. Kepler built upon both the theoretical concept of sun-centeredness advanced by Copernicus and his own expert mathematical analysis of the extensive observational data of the planets that he inherited from Tycho Brahe, to introduce a modern scientific perspective that included planetary laws of motion. Newton later introduced the idea of a universal law of gravitation, with analysis consistent with Kepler's three planetary laws. These concepts represented a sweeping revolution in which the science of astronomy was successfully able to overthrow notions of the heavens that dated to antiquity, and that were also quite entrenched culturally. It was a revolution that is still felt today.

Today we take for granted that our planet is one of the planets of our solar system that revolve around the sun. On a galactic scale we know that the sun is a star that revolves in a much larger orbit within its galaxy (the Milky Way), and that billions of other galaxies exist, with uncounted other stars and planets. From a purely statistical perspective, the evidence of astronomy would appear to contradict any notions of Earth's special placement in the universe. This has been linked, in the modern mind-set, with a corresponding downgrading of the Earth's supposed importance.

Twentieth- and twenty-first-century thinkers have tended to patronize as rather silly and ignorant the notion that man could ever have considered his terrestrial home as the center of things, or that the Earth could in any way be related to a reason for the universe's existence. Surely, it is suggested, there are other races of intelligent beings, perhaps more advanced than us, somewhere out in the expanses of the cosmos, and we are just a part of the mix. This so-called "universe view" has been romanticized by the pop culture, particularly in the modern myths of movie science fiction with their plenteous alien civilizations that apparently populate every nook and cranny of the universe. While entertaining, these stories are no more accurate than the fables of ancient Greece as regards to any factual content pertaining to the habitability of the universe. Modern atheistic thinkers have dictated that the Earth and universe must be fairly average (4), whatever that is. This philosophical view is denoted by what has come to be known as the "Copernican principle," which summarily prescribes that there is nothing special or central about the Earth, the sun, our solar system or us. Actually, as is often the case with neat little summaries, this one has big problems. As pointed out by Gonzalez and Richards, medieval philosophy considered Earth to be more at the bottom of the universe than at the center, and this view was founded in Greek philosophy and not in Biblical Scripture (5). In refuting Earth-centeredness, some believe they have disproved the Bible. This is absurd. There is, to this author's knowledge, no place in Scripture that says that the Earth is the geometrical or physical center of the universe. For centuries, scientists did not know that the Earth is much smaller physically than the stars. Nor was it appreciated that the Earth is in one particular galaxy out of billions in the universe. Discovering these things caused some to jump to the conclusion that a "scientific" view of the Earth is consistent with the notion that neither the Earth nor us are special. However, astronomical research over the last 50 years or so has tended to refute this view. Discoveries now indicate that the Earth is absolutely unique with respect to the rest of space. In particular, the data indicates that the Earth is particularly well positioned and composed for the support of advanced life (6). The combination of Earth's makeup including chemical and geomagnetic properties, its water cycle, the presence of tectonic plates, its atmospheric constituents, its specific position in the solar system, the sun's position in the galaxy, and the sun's properties with respect to those of other stars, are all just right for life. This is entirely consistent with the Biblical revelation that the Earth was created for a purpose, "to be inhabited," as stated in Isaiah 45:18.

What if, just as the medieval geometric view was a poor misjudgment of the structure of the solar system, galaxy and space, so the modern view of Earth's apparent mediocrity is a severe misjudgment regarding a purposeful creation of God? Creation has tremendous value to us and to God, according to His will and purpose. The phrase "the heavens and the earth" is used in verse one of the Bible, and much of the creation events in chapters one and two of Genesis are focused on what the Lord did on and for the Earth. In the book of Genesis the Bible does not elaborate with details regarding the other planets; evidently, they aren't so important in terms of God's revelation to us. As for the creation of stars, in Genesis 1:16 we find the statement "He made the stars also." The brief nature of the statement perhaps conveys the idea that making the stars was really no big deal for the power of God. The stars are for "signs" (Genesis 1:14), but were apparently also not the central focus of creation. From a Biblical perspective, the Earth appears to be much more important than the stars, and the purpose of the stars appears to be Earth-centered. One of the revealed functions of the heavens is "to declare the glory of God" (Psalm 19:1). If we consider the "center" of creation not so much from a geometric as from a value-centered perspective, then the creation including the Earth has tremendous purpose according to God's design and will. In Matthew 6:10 (NKJV) Christ told us to pray "Your will be done on earth as it is in heaven," indicating the importance of what transpires on earth, with much revolving around Christ and His church. In terms of the large number of stars, some have asked why the waste of so many billions of stars if it is really all just to support mankind?

In response to this, it is interesting that astrophysicists tell us that stars were needed for the manufacture of many of the elements that are required for life (7).

Based on modern astronomy, it would appear that the Earth really is quite special within the universe, in the same sense that a master painting on display at a particular museum could be considered the centerpiece of the museum. The painting is not necessarily at the physical center of the museum. However, there is a controlled lighting system, humidity system, security system, and access protection. The building encloses it. The corridors go by the painting and signs point the way to it. It is displayed prominently and is advertised. The view of a high and unique value to the earth is revealed in Scripture and supported by modern physics and astronomy. We really are on a very special piece of real estate in the expanse of creation, one that is central if not at the center, and that has been tended to by a very special Hand. Certainly we can agree with the Psalmist who said "The earth is the Lord's, and the fullness thereof" (Psalm 24:1 (KJV)).

10

THE SKILLFUL CREATION

"He made the heavens skillfully." (Psalm 136:5 (HCSB))

*"Is not God in the height of the heaven?
And see the highest stars, how lofty they are!
And you say, 'What does God know?'" (Job 22:12-13)*

The previous chapter presented an alternative to the several-centuries old "Copernican principle," and pointed out that this view, which entails a characterization of the creation that tends to de-emphasize any suggestion that the Earth, its neighborhood, or even the heavens themselves are somehow special or unique, is at best only an assumption by elements of the scientific community. In this chapter we offer some of the evidence from cosmology and astronomy that supports a non-Copernican* (i.e. we really are special) view of the universe that is the result of a very skillful creative act by God as communicated in Psalm 136:5 (see above).

In the last century and continuing into the current one, scientists have begun to discover fundamental characteristics of the universe that point in the direction of a wonderfully and masterfully crafted creation. One aspect of any device that suggests that skill was required in its construction is the amount of fine-tuning involved for its successful operation. No violin can be tuned randomly and be suitable to be played at a concert. Likewise, no one would believe that a well-tuned musical instrument is a product of chance. Philosopher Robin Collins likens the universe we live in to a system that has dials that need to be "set" to exquisitely precise values in order to function (1). Only an extremely knowledgeable Master would be able to properly set the dials. In fact, whoever set the dials would virtually have to be the Creator based on the level of expertise involved. Cosmological consequences of exquisite fine-tuning are now known to science. This is directly contrary to our modern, preconceived

---

* Note that the term non-Copernican in this context refers exclusively to the baggage associated with the philosophical "Copernican principle" and not to the theory of planetary motion about the sun.

notions that the universe is fundamentally random or derived from chance, and so some may tend to dismiss the evidence in spite of its measurable support. Ross points out that a small change of only about two to three percent in the strength of the strong nuclear force would render the universe completely lifeless due to its effect on fundamental atomic bonding (2). The weak nuclear force is also quite finely-tuned for elemental production within stars (3). In terms of chemical interactions, it is known that the masses of electrons and protons are quite delicately balanced with respect to the strength of electromagnetism (4). This balance is just right for all the amazing chemical interactions that allow different materials within the Earth and within us to form. The polarity of the water molecule is just right allowing for a perfect trade-off of solvency properties, vaporization and relative densities of the phases of water. The amounts of carbon and oxygen, both vital for life, are also narrowly dependent on their nuclear energy level ratio. If this ratio were to be larger, then there would be too little oxygen; whereas if it were smaller, there would be too little carbon for life (5). We observe that the bonds of carbon and oxygen molecules are for the most part nonreactive at normal room temperature, so that fires don't usually ignite spontaneously, while the same chemical affinities are able to support the demanding oxygen and carbon related chemical reactions that occur within living organisms (6). The properly stabilized biochemical reactions of oxygen are due to the physical and chemical properties of oxygen and the catalytic action of enzymes. These highly specific proteins accelerate beneficial reactions but limit potentially dangerous overreactions, and utilize specific metals that themselves have very special chemical and electronic orbital properties (7). These are just a few examples of the highly skillful aspects of the creation that we for the most part take for granted, and yet which are constantly at work both within us and in the world around us.

In summary, we assert that an honest consideration of the preciseness and delicacy required of the constants of nature points to a Designer of incomprehensible skill. The evidence from astrophysics, cosmology and biochemistry indicates strongly that the laws and constants of nature are not of such a character that "just any" values or strengths or properties would suffice. In Romans 1:20 the Scripture seems to indicate that our observations should lead us to glorify God, saying "His invisible attributes are clearly seen, being understood by the things that are made, even His eternal power and Godhead, so that they are without excuse." So, the next time you look under the hood of a hot new car and admire the marvelous engineering design that went into the 390 hp engine, or marvel at all the things your new cell phone can do, you might consider that the design of the universe took infinitely more intentional skill and wisdom than that nice car or phone. And, the One who fashioned the universe is also the One "in whose hand thy breath is" (Daniel 5:23 (KJV)).

11

THE PRAISING CREATION

"Praise the Lord! Praise the Lord from the heavens;
Praise Him in the heights! Praise Him, all His angels;
Praise Him, all His hosts! Praise Him, sun and moon;
Praise Him, all you stars of light!
Praise Him, you heavens of heavens,
And you waters above the heavens!" (Psalm 148:1-4)

"Then, as He was now drawing near the descent of the Mount of Olives, the whole multitude of the disciples began to rejoice and praise God with a loud voice for all the mighty works they had seen, saying: 'Blessed is the King who comes in the name of the Lord! Peace in heaven and glory in the highest!'

"And some of the Pharisees called to Him from the crowd, 'Teacher, rebuke your disciples.' But He answered and said to them, 'I tell you that if these should keep silent, the stones would immediately cry out.'" (Luke 19:37-40)

"Let music swell the breeze, and ring from all the trees Sweet freedom's song: let mortal tongues awake;
Let all that breathe partake;
Let rocks their silence break, the sound prolong." Samuel Smith (verse 3 of "My Country 'Tis of Thee," 1832)

In some profound manner there is built into the essence of creation the capacity to "Praise Him," the "Him" referred to being the Lord Himself. This is a proper response by the creation to its Creator, as declared in the book of Psalms: "Let them praise the name of the Lord, for He commanded, and they were created" (Psalm 148:5). The creation is thus responsive in praise to the Almighty. To some this may appear as pure silliness or at best poetic rhetoric, but this objection is the natural mind presenting its prejudices. The book of 1Corinthians tells us "But the natural man does not receive the things of the Spirit of God, for they are foolishness to him; nor can he know them, because they are spiritually discerned" (1Cor. 2:14). One may wonder in what manner the heavens actually do "Praise the Lord." It is certain that they do as the Scripture informs us. We reject all pantheistic* views as foreign to orthodox Christianity. Perhaps, as a metaphor, one aspect of praise may be that as a picture, let us say a masterpiece, gives credence to the genius of the painter, so do the heavens and the entire creation give glory to the majesty of the Creator. However, this may not encompass the full scope of active praise that the Scripture apparently describes.

The passage from the gospel of Luke chapter 19 in which Christ says that the "stones would immediately cry out" simply cannot be got around. We are faced here with a choice of whether to believe Christ or not. He does not appear to be speaking figuratively or allegorically in giving the remark, for it was in response to complaints that the people were giving Him literal praise as He entered Jerusalem. Here is where it is necessary to receive the kingdom of God as a little child, as the Lord insisted that we must. Our modern, Western, scientifically oriented mindset will utterly fail us at this point; it is only faith that comprehends this matter. The creation is absolutely subject to the Creator, and also to the purposes of the Creator. Jesus said that "the Scripture cannot be broken." Christ's triumphal entry into Jerusalem was an event that was in fulfillment of the prophecy in Zechariah 9:9, and because the Scripture "cannot be broken" according to Christ in John 10:35, there

---

* Pantheism refers to views that tend to view the physical world as a part of God; such views are never supported in the Bible.

had to be the "rejoicing" spoken of in the prophecy. Jesus said that there would have had to be praise, with no exception possible. If the people had not praised Christ, the rocks would have immediately done so as Christ indicated.

12

THE COMPLEXITY CHASM

*"And you forget the Lord your Maker,
Who stretched out the heavens
And laid the foundations of the earth..." (Isaiah 51:13)*

"To whom will you liken Me, and make Me equal And compare Me, that we should be alike?" (Isaiah 46:5)

"Now the serpent was more cunning than any beast of the field which the Lord God had made." (Genesis 3:1)

Science, upon coming to a more sophisticated understanding of the notion of complexity and of its manifest presence within biological systems, has run up against a vast mathematical chasm of "complexity distance," so to speak, between what is observed at any point in the natural but nonliving world and what is regularly seen in the living world of nature. It is now known that huge amounts of information are contained within the chemistry of the cell. This vast space in complexity between the structures and mechanisms abiding in the living and nonliving realms was not truly appreciated in Darwin's day, and to this day the implications seem to be swept into a corner by many evolutionary biologists. Nineteenth-century primitive notions of the cell as relatively bland units seem so naive now as to appear almost comical. Electron micrographs are able to reveal a myriad of subparts of the cell, each amazingly precise and highly complicated from a biochemical perspective. And yet the simple cell model is the intellectual framework within which Darwinian evolution was concocted (1), but which we now know to be the absolute antithesis of reality. In fact, actual cells are extremely complex systems that contain many highly specific, unique and interesting subparts. Explanations of small-scale changes of species that are firmly established observationally lead to a well-grounded theory of "microevolution." Modest changes within species can and do occur. However, the extrapolation of this process to large-scale speciation or "macroevolution" presents problems that are not supported by actual evidence, requiring multiple evolutionary leaps over unfathomable complexity distances. Because supposed instances of macroevolutionary speciation of large animals are relegated to the distant past, there is actually no way to demonstrate that natural selection was the agent of change. As Michael Denton points out, there is historical precedent for extreme caution in extrapolating scientific theories beyond the limited domain of their actual experimental validation (2). To this day, the modern version of Darwin's theory relies on a sort of faith that natural selection, unguided and without a running start, could have leaped these immense chasms of complexity over and over again, something like a desert turtle taking a single running leap over the Grand Canyon. According to Michael Behe, the sorts of multiple sequential increments required to construct the complex entities encountered within cells has not been shown to be something that natural selection has ever been capable of producing (3).

William Dembski has proposed that the natural world obeys a law of conservation of information (4). This says that information cannot be had by any combination of natural laws and chance working in concert. A particular mode of information that he refers to is called "complex specified information." An example would be Mount Rushmore. Although there are many natural, chance patterns etched into the faces of all the mountains of the world, and although some of them might look a bit like real faces, nobody would ever ascribe the obvious faces of Washington, Lincoln,

Jefferson and Theodore Roosevelt on Mt. Rushmore to the random workings of chance via wind, rain and erosion on the rocks. This skepticism would be upheld even if we knew nothing of the history of the magnificent sculpture. The information contained in the pattern of the mountains, with unmistakable resemblance to these famous U.S. Presidents, is just too improbable for a chance occurrence and therefore we conclude that they required intelligence to produce. A specification in terms of a pattern or design is implicit in terms of the sculpted outcome, and the specification followed by its realization is far too complex and specific to be attributed to any non-intelligent cause.

The methods and mathematics of reliably recognizing intelligent causes has advanced in the last 25 years. Dembski reports that his formal tool for recognizing intelligent causes is 100% correct in terms of no false positives when the actual source is known (5). This is a remarkable claim. So, when the specification-complexity method detects design in an observation where the source is not known, design theorists insist that the conclusion ought to be taken seriously based on the evidence. To assert otherwise would not be scientifically credible or logically consistent.

Addressing the religious people of Athens of his day, the apostle Paul proclaimed to them "God, who made the world and everything in it..." (Acts 17:24). In his address Paul told the Athenians that they were "very religious" but were also very ignorant. Today, we see tremendous complexity which cannot be accounted for naturally. However, the high priests of science, the university professors and guardians of orthodoxy at the National Academy of Sciences, along with the popular-science periodical editors, teach us to keep believing that information in the cell is explainable without recourse to a Creator – that somehow, mysteriously, nature has summarily violated the conservation of information principle many times. However, the known complexity chasm between naturally caused events involving law or contingency and the marvelously complex biological systems that we see in the natural world is extremely wide, and is apparently getting wider as our knowledge of these systems advances. Yet, we are told that science urges, nay demands that we must make a leap of faith into exclusive naturalism. Many people have made this leap and continue to make it, accepting that chance and natural selection are the source of all of the biological world's wondrous and intricate inner workings. Some, however, continue to regard this as an irrational and dangerous leap, given the actual facts of modern biology.

Essentially, to insist that natural causes fully suffice for the observed complexity in the biological arena is a form of religious belief – a faith in naturalism, based on the assurances of experts, but not supportable with airtight or even compelling evidence. A much more rational step of faith is to ascribe glory to the Creator who has declared His work of designed creation in the Scriptures, told us in the Scriptures that He is the source of all life, and personally revealed

Himself in Jesus Christ according to Biblical prophecy that can be verified to be 100% accurate. We agree with the Scripture that tells us: "O Lord, how manifold are Your works! In wisdom You have made them all." (Psalm 104:24)

13

THE AGING CREATION

*"Of old You laid the foundation of the earth,
And the heavens are the work of Your hands.
They will perish but You will endure;
Yes, they will all grow old like a garment;
Like a cloak You will change them,
And they will be changed." (Psalm 102:25-26)*

"For the creation was subjected to futility, not willingly, but because of Him who subjected it in hope; because the creation itself also will be delivered from the bondage of corruption into the glorious liberty of the children of God. For we know

that the whole creation groans and labors with birth pangs together until now." (Romans 8:20-22)

The writer of Psalm 102 tells us that "the heavens ... will perish" and "will all grow old like a garment." The apostle Paul gives us further insight in his epistle to the Romans when he says that creation is in a form of "bondage of corruption," which may be viewed as a reference to the effects of the second law of thermodynamics on the physical realm. A modern scientific concept of the second law of thermodynamics includes the notions of thermodynamically irreversible processes in which entropy, or disorder, increases (1). Spontaneous processes, those that actually occur at finite rates in the universe, are irreversible in the thermodynamic sense. Thus, entropy increases over time according to the second law. This principle was in no way obvious to scientists for many years. In fact, according to Gonzalez and Richards, the dominant Aristotelian view held for centuries that the elements of the heavenly realm were unchanging in their basic form (2).

The second law of thermodynamics, in general terms, states that closed physical systems tend inexorably to increasing disorder over time. The physical concept of increased entropy is associated with reduced order (3). A consequence of this law is that there is less and less energy available for useful work of any form. As an analogy take for example a battery-driven watch. As it runs there is less total chemical energy available to drive the action of the watch, and in time the watch will stop. This same principle applies broadly to the physical creation from its largest to smallest components. In space we observe the process of star burning. There have even been recorded historical observations of stars reaching a supernova stage, exploding and ceasing to be stars. Both star burning and supernova explosions are processes of entropy increase, all being driven by the prior available energy and orderliness in the stars. Once that energy and order is used up, it cannot, by any known natural process, be retrieved again for useful work.

One of the most direct evidences of the elderliness of the universe and Earth derives from the relative abundances of naturally occurring radioactive elements or nuclides. According to Hayward (4) there are radioactive nuclides that have relatively short half lives (i.e. less than 50 million years), and those nuclides are all missing from the Earth. On the other hand, naturally occurring nuclides with half lives of about 80 million years and above are all present in some abundance on the Earth. One can think of these as candles that burn at different rates; the fast-burning candles are all gone but the slower burning ones are still around to some extent. This gives scientists one means of establishing the antiquity of the Earth (there are numerous others). This and other methods indicate that the Earth is not in a state of pristine youth. It is without a doubt aged; and, this phenomenon was predicted by Scripture centuries ago in the passage from Psalm 102 quoted previously. Even if, as some suggest, the physical decay rates of the radioactive elements were faster in the past so that absolute years are not able to be accurately found by use of radioactive decay calculations, the evidence that the universe has aged from its original state still remains. In other words the universe, sun and Earth are not young in terms of measurements of physical decay, no matter how old their age in years.

The laws of thermodynamics are based on observation and experiment (5). The second law of thermodynamics and hence the aging process is irreversible as far as we know from observational physics. Some have made predictions of the future based only on physical projections and conclude that the universe is going to run down like a wind-up clock. Only a certain number of stars exist in the universe, and they can only burn for only so long. Knowing this, astronomers can project onward to a hypothetical time when our universe would be like the faintly glowing embers of yesterday's campfire. What does this imply in terms of the ultimate purpose for our lives and individual endeavors? Can there be any real purpose to a universe, or to the lives that reside within it, when all there is to the future is eternal decay without hope? What of knowledge, sacrifice, morals, greatness, love, hate, desire, world records? How substantial are our greatest accomplishments? To really face this question is to face up to the necessity for an eternal soul. Nothing else makes sense. Otherwise, as the apostle Paul said in 1 Corinthians 15:32 "Let us eat and drink, for tomorrow we die." Clearly the apostle had comprehended this great question, and his answer was that there is a resurrection of the dead and, as the prophet Isaiah said, "a new heavens and a new earth" (Isaiah 65:17). So, we must never think that this life is a self-enclosed system of physical acts along with their temporary rewards. Jesus taught in His lessons about later rewards that those who mourn now will laugh then, and those who give in secret now will be rewarded by God then. This world in and of itself has nothing lasting that it can offer. The physical creation is by its very essence non-lasting, but the wise person will realize this and not place his or her true hopes in this life. The apostle John stated "And the world is passing away, and the lust of it; but he who does the will of God abides forever" (1 John 2:17).

The Lord has a surprise for those who believe that the universe will run down like a clock and ultimately cool off like an open oven. As the apostle Peter said: "knowing this first: that scoffers will come in the last days, walking according to their own lusts, and saying, 'Where is the promise of His coming? For since the fathers fell asleep, all things continue as they were from the beginning of creation.' For this they willfully forget: that by the word of God the heavens were of old, and the earth standing out of water and in the water, by which the world that then existed perished, being flooded with water. But the heavens and the earth which are now preserved by the same word, are reserved for fire until the day of judgment and perdition of ungodly men...But the day of the Lord will come as a thief in the night, in which the heavens will pass away with a great noise, and the elements will melt with fervent heat; both the earth and the works that are in it will be burned up"(2 Peter 3:3-8,10). According to this Scripture, the Lord Himself will suddenly bring this age of His creation to an end. However, the book of Hebrews states "Jesus Christ is the same yesterday, today, and forever" (Hebrews 13:8). For true hope to exist, it must be in something that is not subject to decay. Jesus said in John 8:58 "Most assuredly, I say to you, before Abraham was, I AM." It is therefore absolutely certain that Christ does not change or decay, can die no more (Revelations 1:18), and is not subject to the law of entropy. For the soul that looks beyond this creation to Christ, there is joy and not gloom, peace and not anxiety, love with meaning and not mere random acts. The apostle Paul declares "while we do not look at the things which are seen, but at the things which are not seen. For the things which are seen are temporary, but the things which are not seen are eternal" (2 Corinthians 4:18).

14

THE CONSERVATIVE CREATION

"And the Lord God formed man of the dust of the ground..." (Genesis 2:7)

"And the Lord God caused a deep sleep to fall on Adam, and he slept; and He took one of his ribs, and closed up the flesh in its place. Then the rib which the Lord God had taken from man He made into a woman, and He brought her to the man." (Genesis 2:21-22)

The great French chemist Lavoisier is credited with coming up with the notion of conservation of mass.

He performed careful experiments to show that in the process of chemical transformation no mass is actually created or lost, only transformed into different compounds. This surprising (at the time) notion helped lay the foundation for modern chemistry and physical science. In fact the modern laws of physics give high status to notable conservation laws, including (among others) conservation of mass-energy in the first law of thermodynamics, conservation of momentum in mechanics, conservation of electric charge in electromagnetism, and conservation of angular momentum in quantum mechanics. Principles of conservation give scientists and engineers a way of analyzing things with great precision, since the corresponding mathematical statements are ones of equality. This thereby allows analysis of conditions before and after an event, reaction or process of some type. The first law of thermodynamics, which essentially states that mass-energy is conserved, is a generalization of the conservation of mass law and is a basic and very powerful statement of a conservation principle that is apparently built into the universe. Miracles may violate this law but apparently nothing else of a physical nature does.

The Lord created the heavens, the Earth, light, the firmament, and the heavenly lights as described in the initial verses of the book of Genesis. It would appear, however, that the Creator wished to not subsequently reinvent from scratch each and every detail of His creation. In the creation of man and woman we see an application of conservation in the means of creation.

First the Lord used the dust of the ground to create man rather than creating him from nothing, and then used a "rib" from the man from which He fashioned the first woman. Going on in Genesis, in the Scriptural account of the flood, we are told how God preserved human beings and animal species by means of an ark. Of course, it would have been entirely within God's power to re-create the animals, thus saving Noah the immense effort of constructing such an enormous vessel. However, this was not God's method. It seems that the Lord, having completed the six days of creation, wanted to maintain His creation, including man and beasts, for the time period of Earth's current existence.

The structure and mechanisms of the biological creation include variations of analogous or similar forms that pervade nature (1). Similarity of organs, systems and structures among different species is undeniable; in fact, it is one of the characteristics that is most striking in the animal and plant kingdoms, both living and fossilized. Many examples of functional similarity exist between the organic systems of man and animals, (e.g. the immune system, the circulatory system, the nervous system, etc.). At least one modern-day advantage to this similarity is that scientists can use animal models to help develop successful new drugs and treatments that benefit millions of people. We also see a conservative nature in the design of the skeletons of vertebrates, with similar structures that are applied to different purposes. Witness the hands of primates, the wings of birds and the flippers of dolphins. Each is extremely well suited to its own purpose and yet each bears structural resemblance to the others. At the biochemical level there are also quite a few similar molecules over the diversity of nature.

It would appear that much like the composer of a symphony develops and refines musical themes over its several movements, so has the Creator taken common themes and added variations in the kingdoms of life on Earth. Dembski and Wells in their text on biological design discuss an analogy of biological design to engineering design based on subpart functionality (2). Reuse and application of subsystems and partial designs is a well-known principle in engineering, and the Lord appears to be the first Engineer to have used it. The similarities between both extinct and living animals can be viewed as support for, and entirely consistent with, the use of common design-based forms in creation rather than indirect evidence of natural selection. Darwinism entails an attempt to explain the similarities in the animal and plant kingdoms using an entirely naturalistic approach. Early in the development of Darwinism there was a theory that "ontogeny recapitulates philogony," essentially saying that the stages of embryonic development mimic the stages of evolution of a species. As pointed out by Nelson, however, the facts of biology do not support this evolutionary construct (3). Thus this theory of recapitulation turns out to be false—it appears to have been an imposition of a form of expected conservation to the natural world, if evolution were true. This is one historical example of a failed prediction by evolutionists. In fact, evolution cannot predict which species will evolve from a prior one. It instead tries to assign histories to the past development of species, but these can never be specifically proven even in cases where there is supposedly a multitude of evidence such as the development of mammals from therapsids (4). In many cases there is conflicting evidence, often leading to dualing theories of descent, and no possible means of direct confirmational proof of the various claims of its proponents.

The theory of evolution has another dilemma; it points to so-called homologous structures as proof of common descent, but when such structures are obviously not based on common descent the theory's advocates cook up a term called "convergent evolution," which is nothing more than saying that the facts aren't consistent with common descent and therefore evolution came up with a wild coincidence. How many wild coincidences are we supposed to admit before wondering if there is something not quite right about all these speculations? A well-known example of supposed convergent evolution is the eyes of octopi and human beings, which are similar but are not believed, even by evolutionists, to derive their similarity from common ancestry. On the contrary, those who hold to a theory of design by the Creator can look to similarity as supportive of the notion of a creation that has a certain amount of conservative design principles built into it by the Creator. There is absolutely no conflict with this theory and the world of nature. The world of microbiology has, to scientists' surprise, been inundated with examples of so-called "convergent evolution" of biochemically similar or identical molecules and/or functional capacities that are again not theorized, even by evolutionists, to be related by common descent. This, as pointed out by Rana, was an entirely unexpected consequence of research to those who based their views on evolutionary theory (5). However, similar biochemical molecules and functions are entirely consistent with a Biblical view of creation.

The theme of conservation in nature and biology seems to convey a characteristic regarding the way that the Creator designed His creation to exist according to normal natural processes. Physical events normally follow a set of laws that include conservation of various fundamental entities. However, conservation does not preclude miracles or God's intervention, since conservation laws only describe the physical realm when supernatural influences are not operating to override the natural. We see in Scripture that God's power can and does at times intervene within the physical realm. God's miracle power is not a subject of physical science (nor could it be). The Lord shows us that in performing miracles He may sometimes choose to not re-create things, as in the matter of the quail in Numbers 11:31 where He apparently caused an existing flock of birds to provide for His people. A tendency towards conservation even in the midst of miracles is shown in the New Testament when Jesus transformed water to wine rather than creating wine out of nothing. However, depending on His will, at times the

Lord apparently still creates new matter, as when Christ multiplied the loaves and fishes (Matthew chapter 14 and John chapter 6). However, we also see that afterward, He who could multiply the loaves and fishes at will was not willing to waste the products of His miraculous power, as He commanded after the miracle to "Gather up the fragments that remain, so that nothing is lost"(John 6:12). How much more, regarding not just loaves and fishes, but the souls that He has created, is the Lord "not willing that any should perish, but that all should come to repentance" (2 Peter 3:9).

15

THE DUST OF CREATION

"Then God said, "Let the earth bring forth the living creature according to its kind..." (Genesis 1:24)

*"For dust you are,
And to dust you shall return." (Genesis 3:19)*

*"O Lord, how manifold are Your works!
In wisdom You have made them all." (Psalm 104:24)*

The Character of Creation

"Oh, the depth of the riches both of the wisdom and knowledge of God! How unsearchable are His judgments and His ways past finding out!" (Romans 11:33)

It is instructive both scientifically and morally to consider the humble nature of our bodily constituents. Our bodies are, both Biblically and scientifically, dust. It doesn't sound too impressive. We might think of the dust that we wipe clean from our furniture or the dirt we wash off of our car. In fact, the dust or dirt that we are made up of is indeed quite common, but has hidden within its molecular structures a vast richness of quality with regard to its specific chemical potentialities. The characteristics of the various combinations of elements of this world continue to be studied extensively by chemists and biochemists. Perhaps they could also be termed "dustologists." More and more they are finding out just how special the dust is. In fact, the discoveries of chemistry over the past two hundred years with respect to the requirements of life point to a purposeful creation that allows for both the elaborate structures and amazingly intricate functions of life.

The elements can be ordered in what is known in chemistry as the "periodic table." This ordering is according to similarity in the chemical attributes of the various elements; for example, certain elements such as helium, neon and argon are almost completely inert (i.e. react chemically only with great difficulty), and thus are included in one group. Other elements such as the alkali metals react vigorously with almost all nonmetals and are therefore not found in their elemental states in nature. The mere existence of such a thing as a periodic table of the elements is extremely remarkable and quite useful to mankind. Chemists have learned that the elemental relationships and tendencies toward periodic patterns of reactivity are in fact related to the fundamental laws of physics, with electron orbitals, which permit chemical reactions, the result of allowed orbital states based on quantum-mechanical rules. Thus the laws of quantum mechanics, which are perfect for star formation and electromagnetic energy transport, are also ideal for the chemistry of life.

The more we learn about chemistry, the more amazing the overall structure appears. A number of common elements and compounds have very highly specific properties pertaining to the structure and function of life (1). For example, it turns out that carbon is perfect for life's fundamental chemical structural bonds, oxygen and hydrocarbons perfect for the reactions required for the metabolic energy requirements of the cell, the peculiar combination of two hydrogen atoms and a single oxygen atom (better known as water) is ideal for life's internal environment and solutions, and carbon dioxide as a gas by-product of oxidative metabolism is just right in terms of its weak acidic buffering in solution. Iron and copper have properties that are ideal for control of oxygen-based chemical reactions, and a number of trace metallic elements specifically support many special functions of biochemistry. The book of Jeremiah states that "He made the earth by His power, established the world by His wisdom, and spread out the heavens by His understanding" (Jeremiah 51:15 (HCSB)). We see in the capacities of these chemical substances that extreme wisdom and knowledge was required for their creation, for any deviations from the apparently perfect properties of these substances would have prevented the possibility of life (2).

As alluded to above, carbon-based chemistry, with a vast scope of variations (just pick up any textbook on biochemistry to get an idea of the expanse of this subject), is the chemical basis upon which all earthly life exists. Carbon is incredibly well suited as the substrate element for life (3). The flourishing world of organic chemically-based life requires thousands of individual molecules, many of which are only possible given some extremely tight constraints on the laws of physics and chemistry. Proteins, nucleic acids (DNA, RNA), enzymes and basic sugars, carbohydrates and fats are all carbon based, and each are fundamental for the processes of life. Further, carbon has chemical properties that are perfectly suited to the solvent properties of liquid water. In terms of thermodynamic properties, carbon's molecules are able to react using a relatively small amount of energy, yielding an extremely large variety of diverse products. There is no other element that is as suitable for the mass storage and release of biochemical energy as carbon. Carbon-based oxidation allows the controlled release of tremendous amounts of chemical energy that is available for the processes of life. Carbon is able to form diverse protein molecules that have very specific binding properties, from which most of our bodies are constructed. Proteins are involved in movement (muscles), healing (the immune system), nerves (the brain's function), cleansing (the filtration systems), environmental protection (skin), chemical control (enzymes), transport mechanisms within cells, and systemic signaling, feedback and control with hormones. The highly precise carbon-based enzymes accelerate and control precisely orchestrated cascades of biochemical reactions so that life processes within our bodies are able to perform activities that otherwise (i.e. without enzymes) would not be possible at the needed rates. The function of all proteins is determined by their three-dimensional shape, which results from the specific sequence of individual amino acids. This sequence is constructed using peptide chemical bonds that are relatively strong. However, the correct three-dimensional geometry is also held in place by weaker bonds that are also vital for life's function. The chemical coexistence of both of these types of bonds, leading to the extensive and widely diverse chemical geometric structures observed in nature, is a consequence of the potential of carbon's amazingly unique chemical properties. The highly precise joint functionality of different types of bonds inspires awe at the wisdom of the Creator. What God said of the Earth in Isaiah, that He "...did not create it in vain; Who formed it to be inhabited" (Isaiah 45:18), certainly applies well to carbon.

The chemistry of life centrally involves information processing: the storage, expression and replication of huge amounts of information. The carbon-based biopolymers DNA and RNA are the primary handlers of this life-information. These molecules do not occur naturally outside of living organisms. They are highly special in several ways. One of their most amazing properties, discovered in the mid-20th century, is that they are able to store and transfer massive amounts of biological information by means of a chemical code. Codes are algorithmic means by which a designer can specify information for a system, or by which information is transmitted over a channel. In our world where the internet and texting cell phones are ubiquitous, the concept of coded information seems rather modern. However, coded information has, it would appear, existed from the beginning of the creation of reproducing life on Earth (and the source of the apparently optimized genetic code has never been satisfactorily explained by evolutionary theory).

In order for any life-based "dust" in the form of chemical compounds to exist anywhere in the universe, it appears more and more that the laws of chemistry must have been precisely tuned. As mentioned above, chemical reactions are results of the electron orbital properties of the various elements. The fine structure constant (called alpha) relates the relativistic, quantum and electric strengths. Its value of about 1/137 is apparently just right for chemistry. According to Barrow and Webb, small changes in this value would lead to momentous consequences for the universe (4). They point out that a lower value of alpha would change the density of solid atomic matter, change the sensitivity of molecular bonds to temperature, and increase the number of stable elements in the periodic table. A value that is too large, however, would eliminate small nuclei and a value larger than .1 would eliminate carbon altogether. So the "dust" that we are made of is quite contingent on the particulars of chemical-physical laws being just what they are.

The apostle John relates an incident in John chapter 9 of how Jesus healed a man who was blind from birth. At first what Christ did may seem rather odd to us. The Scripture tells us: "He spat on the ground and made clay with the saliva; and He anointed the eyes of the blind man with the clay. And He said to him, 'Go, wash in the pool of Siloam' (which is translated, Sent). So he went and washed, and came back seeing" (John 9:6-7). We see that Christ, the Great Physician, used the dust of this world and his own saliva as the physical implements for healing this man's eyes. The story reminds us of our own physical nature (dust), and where the true power of life abides, not in dust, but in Christ.

16

THE RATIONAL UNIVERSE

"Come now, and let us reason together, saith the Lord: though your sins be as scarlet, they shall be as white as snow..." (Isaiah 1:18 (KJV))

"Oh, the depth of the riches both of the wisdom and knowledge of God!
How unsearchable are His judgments and His ways past finding out!
'For who has known the mind of the Lord?
Or who has become His counselor?'" (Romans 11:33-34)

The Character of Creation

"The Lord by wisdom founded the earth;
By understanding He established the heavens;
By His knowledge the depths were broken up,
And clouds drop down the dew." (Proverbs 3:19-20)

"It is the glory of God to conceal a thing: but the honor of kings is to search out a matter." (Proverbs 25:2 (KJV))

Rational: "Relating to, based on, or agreeable to reason." Merriam-Webster's Collegiate Dictionary (1)

The Scripture tells us in Genesis that man has been given the charter to "fill the earth and subdue it" (Genesis 1:28). The process of "subduing" has, within the last several hundred years, been prefaced by the process of systematic understanding of the physical world. As a consequence, our systems of education and philosophy seem these days to take the position, almost without question, that the world is orderly, comprehensible, and accessible to human reason. Modern scientists generally assume this to be true, perhaps without realizing this assumption's theological roots in Judeo-Christian theology and Biblical revelation.

Clearly science is possible and the world is not totally chaotic, characteristics that are a prerequisite for science as pointed out by Dembski (2). In Genesis 15:5 we are told of an incident between the Lord and Abraham. Scripture tells us "Then He brought him outside and said, 'Look now toward heaven, and count the stars if you are able to number them.'" The command by the Lord to Abraham to "count the stars" implies the ability by Abraham to at least attempt to apply a form of human logic (counting) to the heavenly realm.

By experience and study man has found that the physical laws of nature that pervade the universe are extensive, orderly, non-capricious and stable. There manifestly is an inherent form, order and structure in the physical world that is amenable to human reason. There is no a priori reason, from a purely naturalistic point of view, that this should be so. Atheism combined with reason alone offers no explanation. Of central interest is the source of the rationality that we see in the real natural world. We see examples of a belief in the ultimate rationality of the universe throughout the early history and development of Western science. A number of the primary early developers of modern science (e.g. Copernicus, Galileo, Kepler, Newton and others) held to a belief in a Creator according to the Christian tradition, and their philosophies of nature tended to reflect the characteristics of Biblical revelation. For example, the expectation that Kepler had in seeking to discover laws of planetary motion was undergirded by his confidence in a rational universe due to his confidence in the God of the Bible. One of his biographers emphasizes the fact that Kepler's starting point was not one of unbelief, but instead Kepler stated regarding his pursuits "Man, stretch thy reason hither, so that thou mayest comprehend these things" (3). For Kepler and others, the rationality of science was a consequence of their faith in God.

Dmitri Mendeleyev formulated the concept of an organized table of the elements that was based on observed groupings of related chemical properties. In doing so he was actually able to accurately predict the discovery of "missing" elements such as gallium, germanium and scandium. Such insights would be completely impossible except for an underlying organization and rational structure to the elements themselves. We now know that this structure is due to the allowed electron orbitals of each element that ultimately are based on quantum mechanical rules, electromagnetic force strength, and mass relationships of protons, neutrons and electrons.

In the area of invention, the Wright Brothers did not just haphazardly launch a motorized kite one day; instead, they spent a number of years in careful research into the mechanics of powered flight and optimal wing structure. It was a fundamentally rational research and development plan, based on well-conceived experiments, and a bold confidence that their research could pay off. Moving forward into the latter part of the twentieth century, the moon missions of the 1960s were predicated upon a tremendous amount of knowledge of orbital dynamics, materials science, propulsion, navigation, high-speed powered flight, control systems, electronics, communications, computation and other fields. The fields of biology and medicine have seen revolution after revolution in the last 150 years. In microbiology we are at the point where the marvelous designs of biochemical systems within cells are now beginning to be observed and comprehended. And certainly modern medicine bears small resemblance to that of 200 years ago; we now have crafted prosthetic devices for the disabled, medicines for diabetes, some cures and improvements in the care for cancer, antibiotics that have prolonged the lives of millions, and a host of other treatments for which we are all thankful. All of these collectively testify to the rationality of the created order.

It is interesting to note that the book of Daniel prophesies that "knowledge shall increase" (Daniel 12:4). The realization of this prophesied increase in knowledge in these last days applies to all aspects of physical science, engineering and medicine, and has led to revolutionary changes in what we view as "modern" as opposed to as little as 300 years ago. Our universe is apparently one in which relatively simple and broad laws can be observed to characterize the behavior of physical entities with high precision. That these laws can be discerned by human reason is remarkable. For example, the force of gravity (in Newtonian terms) between two objects can be concisely expressed as $F = G\, m_1\, m_2\, /\, r^2$. This is a beautifully simple and elegant expression. It simply states that the force felt by the objects is a constant (G) times the product of the masses of the two objects, divided by the square of the distance between their respective centers of mass. With this relatively simple expression people found that they were able to accurately solve a wide range of problems regarding both cosmological and earthbound motion. This was a tremendous advance for physics. It is deceptively easy to take the simplicity and universality of the gravitational relationship for granted. What if the Newtonian law of gravity were something else? For example, what if the result did not involve a simple product of their masses, but instead a more complicated relationship? Depending on the form, this could have been be a more difficult law to discover, or we may never have had a chance to even decipher such a law. However, this is not the case (thankfully) for Newtonian gravity, and for many other things as well. It is true that Einstein's general relativity gives a more exact and much more involved solution to gravity, but it also is amenable to human reason and analysis. Indeed, the laws that describe the universe seem to be just within the grasp of our ability to comprehend them.

It is out of a firm confidence in the rationality of the world (even by those who do not acknowledge its creation) by which theories of science are now reviewed and received. Indeed, when there is the appearance of inconsistency either mathematically, logically or with reference to experimentation, it drives the quest for a deeper and better understanding. A well-known example of this is the developmental motivation for quantum mechanics. According to the classical physics at the end of the 19th century, the energy that oscillators emit was calculated to increase with no limit as their frequency increased. This was clearly nonphysical (one term for it was the "ultraviolet catastrophe"), and motivated Max Planck to propose that electromagnetic radiation is quantized, eventually leading to a revolution in physics. This motivating example involved a contradiction between the physically absurd notion of infinite energy (e.g., see Penrose (4)) and experimental observation. Rationality dictated a search for a better answer. A more recent example is in the area of string theory, which has had multiple mathematical versions, all of which were apparently equally valid, thereby motivating intense study to resolve the inconsistencies, some of which have indeed been resolved (5). This is not to say that string theory is even approximately correct or proven, but only that it would never be viewed as correct if it had multiple versions that had not been reconciled. The perceived need for new and better theories has a basis in the confidence of scientists that there exists a fundamental rationality in the physical universe—that mathematical or logical inconsistencies will not exist in correct theories of physics or any other scientific field. Another example is the apparent discrepancy between two very accurate theories of nature, quantum mechanics and general relativity. Currently, the theoretical predictions of quantum mechanics and general relativity clash under hypothetical conditions of very small dimensions and high mass-energy such as those theorized to exist prior to "Planck time"* at the earliest moments after creation. This is motivating study of theories of quantum gravity and string theory to reconcile the predictions.

---

* About 10^{-43} seconds.

An aspect of rational thought that pervades our culture as well as science is that there must be observable evidence in support of an accepted theory of physics. A corollary is that a theory must not violate clear, measurable facts of observation. The reliance on experimental substantiation pervades all of the physical sciences. Thus, experimentalists in physics are quite necessary for the advance of physically grounded theories. And, any theory is only one experiment away from the junk pile, or at least the "back to the drawing board" stage. Historically, a relatively nonmathematically inclined scientist, Michael Faraday, is nevertheless regarded as one of the greatest physicists ever. He aimed to discover the laws that the Creator had put into the creation (6), and succeeded to no small extent with many painstaking experiments and carefully noted observations.

It is unfortunate that more biologists and paleontologists, when considering the scope and domain of the neo-Darwinist theory of evolution, do not apply the same firm evidential principles that physicists insist on, with insistence on experimental verification and lack of observed contradictions, for then creation of new species by natural selection would not be so often promoted as a "fact." For example, the appearance of highly specific phyla and classes at the start of the Cambrian period has not been explained by natural selection to any degree of certainty (7). In the area of biochemistry, Michael Behe has pointed out other serious problems with the theory of natural selection coupled with random mutation due to its inability to account for the presence of "irreducibly complex" entities in the cell (8). Some people object to Behe's argument and think that evolution can indeed explain such things as the blood-clotting cascade and bacterial flagellum, but the fact is that they have not yet explained it in Darwinian terms to the point of a solid proof or in fact any proof at all, and so Behe's objections should be allowed some considerable weight. Instead, proponents of evolution urge us to have faith in their theory (a sort of reverse "god of the gaps" argument for evolution). For some of us our faith is not that great, and I would argue nor should it be. Perhaps this appeal to a hypothetical future reconciliation between Darwinism and the facts of nature may be considered valid as a research program, but not regarded as support for an unproven theory. The Darwinian research program has not succeeded thus far in proving speciation by natural selection (9), its primary goal; it only can explain certain micro-evolutionary changes, and caution is always advised when extrapolating in the sciences to grand conclusions not supported by measured evidence.

Were it not for the fact that the universe seems to be highly rational, any attempts to understand the universe would not be any better than guesswork. One cannot explain this rationality based on the fundamentals of science itself. A summary view of science as the very basis of truth, a view called "scientism" according to Moreland (10), admits to rationality within the universe but can never identify its cause within a closed naturalistic system. To claim, as some appear to do, that science by studying the world is hence a rational enterprise, and that therefore the world is rational when described by science, begs the question of the basis for rationality in either science or the world. On the contrary, the God of the Bible's constancy and truth is a firm and unchanging basis for the rationality that exists in the universe. Examples of this are seen in His words, such as Isaiah 1:18 where He says "Come now, and let us reason together," and in the New Testament where the writer of Hebrews says of the Savior and Messiah "Jesus Christ *is* the same yesterday, today and forever" (Hebrews 13:8). The Creator's character, revealed in Scripture and in Jesus Christ, ultimately provides a basis for rationality in a changing and uncertain world, and provides a rationality that extends above science and beyond this world.

The relationship of man to God and the blessings of God are key elements in our understanding of ourselves, the world and God. Any perception of rationality therefore also entails the necessity that we must ourselves also have the capacity to think rationally. Naturalistic evolution can explain neither why the world obeys rational laws or why humans are able to reason about them. According to Dembski, Einstein's famous quote that "The most incomprehensible thing about the world is that it is comprehensible" is properly regarded as a commentary on the limitations of naturalism (11). It seems that the Lord, in creating us in His image, has gifted us with an ability to reason that, in some sense, is matched to the intellectual and moral challenges that the creation presents us with. We are not monkeys (much as some theories would have us believe), which have never once discovered a law of science, and which, to all appearances, do not contemplate why the sun comes up in the morning or what makes leaves green. We are human; and yet, the very fact that we are constantly learning so much indicates that we have not reached anything approaching a pinnacle of knowledge, and that a proper attitude is one of extreme humility of mind. Our minds have been gifted by God to achieve a gradual and imperfect, and yet actual and progressive, understanding of the natural universe. We see and believe that the universe has a pattern, a form beneath the events, that allows us to delve into its secrets, hidden there for us to discover by the Creator, and to give Him glory thereby.

17

THE CAUSAL CREATION

"In the beginning God created the heavens and the earth." (Genesis 1:1)

"By faith we understand that the worlds were framed by the word of God, so that the things which are seen were not made of things which are visible." (Hebrews 11:3)

"'I, Jesus, have sent My angel to attest these things to you for the churches. I am the Root and the Offspring of David, the Bright Morning Star.'" (Revelation 22:16 (HCSB))

The Character of Creation

"So then gravity may put the planets into motion, but without the divine Power it could never put them into such a circulating motion as they have about the sun; and therefore, for this, as well as other reasons, I am compelled to ascribe the frame of the system to an intelligent Agent..." Isaac Newton (1)

The opening words of the Bible do not explain God; they explain the heavens and the earth. Regarding God's existence, the Holy Scripture informs us in Psalm 90 that "From everlasting to everlasting Thou art God" (Psalm 90:2 (KJV)). Thus we know that God Himself was not created or caused to come into existence. Central to the revelation of the creation of the heavens and the earth is the issue of causality, in that the universe required a Cause. The Scripture tells us that "In the beginning God created the heavens and the earth" (Genesis 1:1), and thus we have a causal explanation for the world in which we live. According to the Bible, God caused all things to exist, and the New Testament in discussing Christ says "All things were made through Him, and without Him nothing was made that was made" (John 1:3). Thus the Scripture tells us that God in Jesus Christ is the first Cause for all that was made, and that God was not created Himself. Neither was Christ created, but is eternally a person of the triune God*. The Biblical

---

* The doctrine of the Trinity embodies the Biblical teaching that there are three persons (the Father, Son and Holy Spirit) eternally existing as one God.

doctrine that the universe was caused to come into existence by God is directly in contrast to other philosophies that suggest a circular or oscillating form of time (2). As regards this physical universe, therefore, perhaps one of the most fundamental theological statements to be made concerning it is that it, its physical characteristics, and its overarching laws constitute a creation. This implies that the universe is not self-existent and did not cause its own existence. From this revelation of Scripture an explanation for our own physical existence derives, and our lives as a consequence have God-given purpose, destiny and meaning.

Developments in science during the last hundred years that pointed the way to, as Dr. Allan Sandage put it, "the modern scientific theory of creation" (3), were nothing short of stunning. The evidence of an expanding universe with linear relationships between distance and expansion rate points to a common origin of all physical entities at some time in the past (4). Modern cosmology hypothesizes a single, unique creation event some approximately 14 billion years ago that was the beginning of both space, time and matter-energy. The current best physical model for the universe is called the Hot Big Bang model (5). However, contrary to what the name implies, this model does not tell us what happened at the precise initial moment of creation (6). It appears that there is a time limit before which physics cannot accurately delve, at about "Planck time" after the creation event, which is an extremely small but finite amount of time after time equals 0. Although speculative mathematical exercises about time before time or multiple universes seem to be proliferating these days, these are in principle not verifiable and thus lack the scientific rigor that experimentally verifiable theories rest on.

The quantum world is different in fundamental ways from what we have been led to expect of reality based on our familiar experiences of cause and effect. There are quantum explanations of a sort where particles move "backwards" in time, and while this seems nonintuitive, it may be an accurate picture of the quantum world. How this affects us is an interesting question, but it does not change the "forwardness" of our macro-level cause and effect observations of the world. And, even the strange world of quantum mechanics can potentially be reconciled to causality. David Bohm in the 1950s put forth an apparently tenable view of quantum mechanics that operates by means of "pilot waves"; in this theory, which is consistent with experimental observation (7), causality is maintained at the expense of strict locality. It may be that the quantum world is entangled within itself so that we cannot clearly define its causes and effects; however, at the macro level, the level at which we live, results remain connected to prior causes that are discernable.

According to Penrose (8), the second law of thermodynamics, which essentially states that there is increasing entropy or disorder in closed physical systems over time, is related to the notional "forward" observations of cause and effect over time that we see every day. The laws of classical physics that deal with motion over time in the macro non-quantum sense are not directional in their treatment of sequences of events (9). That is, there is no reason that event sequences cannot run either "forward" or "backward" according to these laws. However, backward motion is never observed to be the case in the macro or non-quantum world, and this apparently accords with the original very low entropy (or high order) of the state of the universe. Penrose calculated the original entropy of the universe to be so low as to defy any explanation based on random chance (8). Physical implication of such low initial entropy are that macro events continue to move in time in what we regard as forward-time behaviors. God has apparently built into the creation the property of cause-and-effect relationships that allow us to reason about events. This affects all physics and all relationships, leading to a "common sense" rationality of cause and effect. As a result of this characteristic of the creation, we are able to develop ideas about observed effects in terms of their prior causes, even extending to an understanding of the universe itself.

The fact that the universe cannot extend to infinite time in the past is a forceful conclusion of the modern cosmology developed during the 20th century. As pointed out by Craig in (10), the scientific evidence for the beginning of the cosmos came as quite a surprise to the scientific establishment in the early to mid-twentieth century. The news was totally unexpected and not particularly welcome. An infinitely existent universe was the accepted philosophical and scientific view among many if not most naturalistic scientists of the late nineteenth and early twentieth centuries. Those with an evolutionary bent wanted to give evolution as much time (near infinite) as possible to get started. To have that view so completely overthrown in the space of about 50 years was a remarkable shift in paradigms. The "Big Bang" theory, on a broad scale, encapsulates the scientific view that there was a physical beginning to the cosmos, implying a Cause for the universe outside of the physical realm. William Lane Craig discusses the argument for the existence of a Creator of the physical universe in terms of logical necessity as a consequence of its beginning to exist at some point (11). He points out that there is much compelling physical evidence for a beginning of both space and time and that this is necessarily compelling evidence for a Creator who transcends space and time. There have been a number of vigorous attempts to refute the Big Bang model, as discussed by Ross (12). However, none of the alternative theories has been able to successfully explain the observed cosmological evidence as well as the Big Bang theory. In spite of the overwhelming physical evidence for a beginning of creation, skeptics of a true beginning may always be with us, with appeals to undiscovered physical laws, which are, after all, another form of faith. And remember, the laws of physics that presumably must exist prior to, or along with, a physically derived creation "event" are also real, and themselves require an explanation if one adopts a "no beginning" manner of reasoning. While physical evidence points to a beginning, even the best evidence still leaves the necessity of placing our faith in the Creator-as-Creator, and in taking the Biblical revelation of the Lord at His word.

Thus to us the best, most wonderful and most consistent explanation with respect to the physical /cosmological evidence of the beginning is "In the beginning God created the heavens and the earth," as repeatedly taught in the Bible. To orthodox Biblical scholars and Christians of the 18th and 19th centuries, the scientific discovery that the universe had a distinct beginning would have come as no surprise. Christians have always known that. For the Christian of today the discovery is a validation of the Church's historical reliance on Genesis and the other Biblical Scriptures as informative and completely reliable in spite of contrary prevailing "scientific" views.

The Scripture in the book of Romans says that "For since the creation of the world His invisible attributes are clearly seen, being understood by the things that are made" (Romans 1:20). According to the Bible, the consideration that there is no God is a foolish thought. Psalm 14:1 states: "The fool has said in his heart, 'There is no God.'" In the end, all foolishness brings (or causes) damage. Thus in a very real sense the philosophy that rejects God also leads to a very real peril to a person's own soul. Conversely, the followers of Christ may confidently trust in Him who, interestingly enough, is Himself not limited to causality, for He says to His people in Isaiah: "It shall come to pass, That before they call, I will answer..." (Isaiah 65:24).

18

HOME SWEET HOME

*"He waters the hills from His upper chambers;
The earth is satisfied with the fruit of Your works.
He causes the grass to grow for the cattle,
And vegetation for the service of man,
That he may bring forth food from the earth..."
(Psalm 104:13-14)*

*"'Indeed My hand has laid the foundation of the earth...'"
(Isaiah 48:13)*

The Character of Creation

"For thus says the Lord, Who created the heavens,
Who is God, Who formed the earth and made it,
Who established it, Who did not create it in vain,
Who formed it to be inhabited:
'I am the Lord, and there no other...'" (Isaiah 45:18)

On a sweltering summer day in Southern California I am thankful for the window air conditioner that makes our house at least livable. And, when visiting the Eastern United States in the winter I have been very glad to have a warm overcoat, hat and gloves. These locales, though uncomfortable at times, are within the nicely habitable regions of the planet. I realize that there are many other places on the surface of our world that are much worse---that are either too high, too hot, too cold or too dry for much of anything (possibly besides bacteria or some hearty plants) to abide there. In a similar vein, for the last 60 years or so astronomers and physicists have studied what are the conditions and materials that are absolutely necessary for life to exist in the universe. The astronomical evidence shows that the Earth is remarkably amiable to advanced life when compared to the vast possibilities for different conditions that exist in the universe and the range of conditions allowable by known physical law. That the Earth is so marvelously fitted for human habitation is perhaps one of the most pronounced and stupendous characteristics of all creation. For those of us who have watched enough science fiction, we may have the impression that all (or at least many) planets in the universe are of the semi-Earth-like type. We naively expect that nearly any solar system you may choose to visit (if that were possible) would be blessed by at least one planet with a comfortable temperature range, relative geologic stability, a habitable atmosphere, a gentle and stable sun, nutritious plants, a comfortable amount of gravity, water in three states, an atmospheric UV shield and many other favorable factors that contribute to habitability.

It may be considered somewhat of a mystery that the Earth and Venus, which are theorized to have started out rather similarly, turned out so differently. The Earth has retained a life-supporting atmosphere; Venus has a thick atmosphere of primarily carbon dioxide and a surface temperature of 867 degrees Fahrenheit (1), hardly conducive to a nice outing at the beach. In fact, a day at the beach on Venus would be a rather dry experience, as most of the water on Venus has escaped to space. We may tend to ask why isn't Venus more "normal"? The answer is that Venus is probably much more of a normal type of planet, cosmically speaking, than the Earth. In *The Scientific American Book of Astronomy* (2), the authors discuss the seemingly small initial differences between Earth and Venus. They state that Venus may even have had oceans at one time. What happened to Venus so that it now has a surface temperature of hundreds of degrees, an atmosphere that contains sulfuric acid, and no oceans? And how did the surface of the Earth avoid the fate of becoming immensely cold or hellishly hot, and come to be blessed with a plentiful supply of liquid water, an atmosphere that supports life, and its many other favorable attributes? The same book goes on to describe how the early Earth had just the right balance of carbon dioxide and water vapor, along with a greater distance from the sun than Venus, thereby preventing the catastrophic processes that occurred on Venus (3). The Earth's carbon dioxide and water vapor operate as a partially open so-called "window" of solar radiation transmission in the atmosphere, allowing just enough warming but not too much, resulting in a quite hospitable balance involving a number of processes, a balance that has continued to this day through times of meteor impacts, volcanoes, ice ages and everything in between.

The comparison between Earth and Mars is also of interest and shows the drastic effects of moderate distance changes from the sun within the solar system. Whereas Venus is the planet just closer to the sun than Earth, Mars is the next planet farther away. As a result of this Mars is quite cold with little if any liquid water, and a primarily carbon dioxide atmosphere that is less than one percent as thick as Earth's (4). There is evidence, based on now-dry fluvial channels, that liquid water once existed on the red planet (5). However, astronomers do not believe there is currently any liquid water at any time on the surface of Mars (6). The frigid environment, along with ultraviolet radiation from the sun, and the very thin and poisonous atmosphere argue against the possibility of current life on the surface of Mars (7). Speculation exists as to the possibility of endemic or transplanted life in geothermally heated areas of the Martian underground (8). However, there is no evidence that advanced organic life has ever existed on Mars.

Despite its many harsh environments, the Earth still remains the only habitable (for humans and higher animals) place that we know of in the universe. We have an extremely rare (at least in our solar system) supply of liquid, solid and gaseous water that is regarded as an absolute requirement for life (9). We still enjoy in some times and places the "cool of the day" as mentioned in Genesis 3:8. No other solar or observed extrasolar planet even comes remotely close to the habitability of Earth. In fact, the fictional worlds that we see in the movies are really just imaginary extensions of Earth's environment with relatively little (compared to the range of possibilities) tweaking. So many are the environmental requirements for life, so rarely are each jointly satisfied, and so narrow are the boundaries of viability, that it is a wonder from a completely naturalistic point of view that we are here at all. One may ask how commonplace is Earth's combination of life-supporting parameters in the universe. Astronomers Peter D. Ward and Donald Brownlee have investigated this very question (10). Their inquiry, which by no means relies on a Biblical or Christian worldview, discusses the uniqueness of our planet from the perspective of the viability of advanced animal life, and supports their "Rare Earth Hypothesis" that although there may be bacterial-type life on a relatively large scale in the universe, from a purely naturalistic perspective we are most likely to be alone in terms of advanced intelligent life. Astronomer Hugh Ross has an extensive compilation of parameters of the Earth and its galactic neighborhood that must be finely tuned, and in some cases extremely finely tuned, in order for life on Earth to exist (11). The Earth's development has been one that supports advanced life forms such as mammals and, of course, human beings. We see that even our closest planetary neighbors, Mars and Venus, lack even a semblance of advanced life-supporting properties. It turns out that a remarkable balance of the atmospheric percentages of carbon dioxide, oxygen, and nitrogen on Earth has moderated a perfectly controlled greenhouse effect that just maintains a proper temperature, within a narrow range, that is suitable for life. We know that life requires water; however, there is no other planet yet discovered either within or outside of our solar system that has just the proper abundance of liquid water that Earth has been endowed with. The presence of a large amount of water on the Earth is of particular Biblical importance, as indicated in Genesis 1:9: "Then God said, 'Let the waters under the heavens be gathered together into one place, and let the dry land appear'; and it was so." Evidently this is a blessing not to be taken lightly, and cosmically may be much rarer than the large volume of water on our planet might lead us to otherwise suppose.

Special qualities of the Earth with respect to the solar system that are necessary for our existence include the proper distance from the sun, the star type of the sun, and the location of the sun within the Milky Way galaxy (14). For each of these parameters there seems to be a very narrow range of values that allows for a habitable Earth. Other special characteristics of the Earth involve its elemental constituents (12). For example, the presence of radioactive elements such as uranium is historically important in generating heat and powering tectonic activity that is essential for maintaining a stable environment (13). Though not ever explored directly, it would appear that the Earth is special down to its very core, which produces a fairly rare but absolutely necessary protective magnetic field (15). The proper amount of sulfur combined with iron is necessary to maintain a circulating liquid iron core necessary for magnetic-field generation. The Scripture even makes special mention of the "foundations of the earth" indicating that it is a result of the direct activity of God: "Where were you when I laid the foundations of the earth? Tell Me, if you have understanding." (Job 38:4)

In the Biblical books of Exodus through Numbers, the Lord continually promises the children of Israel that He is bringing them into a land of milk and honey, of fruit and blessings. And while we are enjoined to not love this world or the things that are in it, it is evident that the Lord delights in blessing His people and even those who are not yet His people, in order to draw men and women to Himself. The Biblical book of The Acts of the Apostles refers to good seasons and food as a witness from God (Acts 14:17). We are reminded in the book of Romans that "the goodness of God leads you to repentance" (Romans 2:4). Yes, the world is clearly fallen and imperfect --- but that does not negate the clear message of creation that God has been good to us and wanted us to have a suitable planet on which to live and serve Him.

19

PURPOSES OF CREATION

"Then God made two great lights: the greater light to rule the day, and the lesser light to rule the night. He made the stars also. God set them in the firmament of the heavens to give light on the earth, and to rule over the day and over the night, and to divide the light from the darkness. And God saw that it was good." (Genesis 1:16-18)

"...according to the eternal purpose which He accomplished in Christ Jesus our Lord..." (Ephesians 3:11)

"For by Him all things were created that are in heaven and that are on earth, visible and invisible, whether thrones or dominions or principalities or powers. All things were created through Him and for Him. And He is before all things, and in Him all things consist." (Colossians 1:16-17)

"Blessed be the God and Father of our Lord Jesus Christ, who has blessed us with every spiritual blessing in the heavenly places in Christ, just as He chose us in Him before the foundation of the world, that we should be holy and without blame before Him in love..." (Ephesians 1:3-4)

Who has not asked themselves the "why" questions of life. Why is there suffering? Why is there evil? Why is there disease and death? Why do things seem unfair? Why am I here? Indeed, the purposes of creation and of life are not easily discerned simply from human experience or logic, and some experiences of life are certain to leave even the wisest person wondering. Sometimes the race is not to the swift, and the battle not to the strong. Some answers are not ever to be found on this side of the veil. And yet, there are revealed purposes in Scripture that, when apprehended by the mind, can serve as a focus for the soul. God has not created a vain creation. In gazing at the night sky and considering the expanse, beauty and power displayed in the heavenly realm, there is a near universal sense of awe and wonder. Perhaps one aspect of this is because the heavens are completely beyond any power of man to control or change; we have never even sent a spacecraft to the nearest star, let alone to the vast company of galaxies. We are observers of the heavens, as Abraham was. Comprehending the sheer number of stars, added to the immense breadth and depth of space, is impossible for our intellect and humbling to our egos. Such observations are able to convince us of a divine Hand (e.g. see Romans 1:20). But what purposes had such a Hand in creating such grandeur? The Scripture does give us some insight into this.

Based on the revelation of the Bible, there are specific purposes assigned for the primary heavenly bodies including the sun and moon and stars. The heavenly lights are described in Genesis 1: "And God said, 'Let there be lights in the firmament of the heaven to divide the day from the night; and let them be for signs, and for seasons, and for days, and years: And let them be for lights in the firmament of the heaven to give light upon the earth'" (Genesis 1:14-15 (KJV)).

So we understand that the sun and the moon are to "give light upon the earth," with "the greater light to rule the day, and the lesser light to rule the night" (Genesis 1:15-16). The sun truly does "rule the day" by providing tremendous amounts of heat and light that keep us alive and warm here on Earth. The moon stabilizes the Earth's tilt, assists in tides, and provides light at night. According to astrophysicists, the stars generate both light and the heavier elements that are required for life, and they have been looked to since antiquity for navigational guidance. Romans 1:20

would seem to enjoin us to observe the creation, with the goal of seeing something of the Creator's attributes of "eternal power and Godhead."

Contrary to the modern notion that "chance" is the cause of the structure of the heavens, with the resulting philosophical implication of nonpurposefulness, we notice a deep sense of ordained purpose on the part of the Creator with regard to the creation in the Scriptures. King David wrote: "When I consider Your heavens, the work of Your fingers, The moon and the stars, which You have ordained, What is man that You are mindful of him, And the son of man that You visit him?" (Psalm 8:3-4)

On Earth itself, the realm of nature works for man's benefit. In Genesis 2:9 we are told "And out of the ground the Lord God made every tree grow that is pleasant to the sight and good for food." The herbs and fruit trees were provided to both man and animals for food in Genesis 1:29-30. After this a purpose for the garden of Eden itself is indicated as a focus of occupation for man: "Then the Lord God took the man and put him in the garden of Eden to tend and keep it" (Genesis 2:15). These purposes for the creation of sustenance, habitation, position and occupation by mankind, established by God at the beginning of creation, continue to the present day.

Consideration of the physical aspects of creation, however wonderful and beautiful they may be, leads to the inevitable conclusion that they are restricted to having only a temporary extent. As the apostle

Peter put it: "All flesh is as grass, And all the glory of man as the flower of the grass. The grass withers, And its flower falls away, But the word of the Lord endures forever." (1 Peter 1:24-25). The second law of thermodynamics is in agreement with this verse, with a message of inevitable decay. However, the vastness and beauty of the heavenly realm suggests something of eternity to our senses, suggesting both temporal and eternal purposes. The book of Ecclesiastes seems to speak of this when it says "Also He has put eternity in their hearts, except that no one can find out the work that God does from beginning to end" (Eccl. 3:11). For the spiritually minded, it is possible to see that the eternal purposes of God are involved in the creation. Christ asked, "For what will it profit a man if he gains the whole world, and loses his own soul?" (Mark 8:36). The matters of the soul transcend this world into the next.

In the Bible we are told that the purposes of creation are focused on, pointed at and centered on Jesus Christ: "All things were created through Him and for Him" (Colossians 1:16). The book of Acts states of Jesus Christ: "Nor is there salvation in any other, for there is no other name under heaven given among men by which we must be saved" (Acts 4:12). For the Christian the purposes of life are accomplished by Christ in us. The apostle Paul had a grasp of this when he said: "Yet indeed I also count all things loss for the excellence of the knowledge of Christ Jesus my Lord, for whom I have suffered the loss of all things, and count them as rubbish, that I may gain Christ and be found in Him, not having my own righteousness, which is from the law, but that which is through faith in Christ, the righteousness which is from God by faith; that I may know Him and the power of His resurrection, and the fellowship of His sufferings, being conformed to His death, if, by any means, I may attain to the resurrection from the dead" (Philippians 3:8-11). In the last chapter of the Bible we are given a divine revelation of Christ Himself where He says "I am the Alpha and the Omega, the Beginning and the End, the First and the Last" (Revelation 22:13). Thus we conclude that there is no true, eternal purpose to or for creation or our individual lives outside of Jesus Christ.

20

THE UNCREATIVE CREATION

*"Who has divided a channel for the overflowing water,
Or a path for the thunderbolt,
To cause it to rain on a land where there is no one,
A wilderness in which there is no man; To satisfy the desolate waste,
And cause to spring forth the growth of tender grass? Has the rain a father?
Or who has begotten the drops of dew? From whose womb comes the ice?
And the frost of heaven, who gives it birth?"
(Job 38:25-29)*

*"Does the hawk fly by your wisdom,
And spread its wings toward the south?" (Job 39:26)*

*"Know that the Lord, He is God;
It is He who has made us, and not we ourselves..."
(Psalm 100:3)*

We are told in Scripture of Jesus Christ that "He was in the world, and the world was made through Him, and the world did not know Him" (John 1:10). In the ancient world the Pharaoh resisted Moses by saying "I do not know the Lord" (Exodus 5:2) and so proceeded to mark his own destiny. We see in the modern world that purely naturalistic interpretations of the created order do not know Him any better, and in doing so only herald their own eventual futility. In criticizing strictly naturalistic or materialist-reductionist views of the world, we certainly do not mean to imply that empiricism*, experiment, and theoretical modeling according to physical and mathematical laws are in any way improper. They are not. In fact they are extremely useful and powerful elements of the scientific method, and empirical evidence actually can in some cases point clearly in the direction of design when all possible causes are not a priori limited to natural explanations (1). The scope of natural causes is inadequate when it comes to evidence for the creative acts of God as they are observed in the natural world. Modern science has been

---

* In this context we generally refer to empiricism to entail a reliance on methods of observation to gain knowledge.

handicapped by the presumption that all is explainable without the Creator, and that all of the amazing complexity that we see is but an illusion of design. Faith and the Biblical Scripture inform us that natural causes alone are insufficient to explain everything we see in the real world, so that the application of strict naturalism is forever blinded to the true Cause of the fundamental characteristics of creation.

Recent years have witnessed great efforts by naturalistic scientists to account for the extreme amount of actual information and complexity present in the realm of biology. All such attempts are, in this author's opinion, totally bankrupt. Yes, there is some self-ordering capacity to nature, but this capacity is minuscule in comparison to the observed order in even the simplest of bacterium, let alone a human brain. Professor Dean Kenyon wrote one of the seminal texts on the possibility of self-ordering, called *Biochemical Predestination.* However, his further studies led him to embrace intelligent design as a much more reasonable theory of the origins of the immense complexity seen in biochemical life (2). Dr. Stephen Meyer points out that the chemical affinities between the constituents of DNA have been shown to not be responsible for the order that is necessary for life (3), and that this order must be a result of information. Mathematician Marcel Shutzenberger put it this way: "No algorithm allows us to understand the complexity of living creatures ...which owe their initial plausibility to the assumption that the physicochemical world exhibits functional properties that in reality it does not possess" (4). C. S. Lewis remarked as to the limits of the created order: "There is something which is directing the universe, and which appears to me as a law...I think we have to assume it is more like a mind...you can hardly imagine a bit of matter giving instructions" (5). Vital Christianity necessarily must take a strong position against those who would seek to distance us from our God by insinuating a godlike "nature" as a necessary creative life force. Contrary to current evolutionist dogma, "nature" has never actually created anything from a single electron to the tiniest bacteria to a star or a galaxy. True, the processes of nature by which matter is continually transformed, with canyons being cut into rock or microevolutionary changes occurring within species, do explain many current and past natural occurrences, but these processes are not watchmakers. "They neither see nor know" as the prophet Isaiah described idols (Isaiah 44:9). We acknowledge that changes happen constantly in nature, but not creative, inventive, life-providing changes. They are the outworking of the natural processes that the Creator has already set in place in the earth. The Bible tells us: "Know that the Lord, He is God; It is He who has made us, and not we ourselves..." (Psalm 100:3). It is God who gave and still gives the real instructions to the universe and to its inhabitants.

21

THE STRETCHED-OUT UNIVERSE

"In the beginning God created the heavens and the earth."
(Genesis 1:1)

"Have you not known? Have you not heard?
Has it not been told you from the beginning?
Have you not understood from the foundations of the earth?
It is He who sits above the circle of the earth.
And its inhabitants are like grasshoppers,
Who stretches out the heavens like a curtain,
And spreads them out like a tent to dwell in."
(Isaiah 40:21-22)

*"He has made the earth by His power,
He has established the world by His wisdom,
And has stretched out the heavens by His discretion."
(Jeremiah 10:12)*

"Thus says God the Lord, who created the heavens and stretched them out..." (Isaiah 42:5)

The Scripture makes a scientifically verifiable statement, in fact a number of statements, that explicitly state that the universe has been expanded or stretched out. Moreover, Isaiah 40:22 uses the present tense when using the verb "stretches," seemingly indicating that the Lord is continuing this action. Most scientists seemed ignorant of this fact up into the early 20th century (1). Their tacit assumption was that the universe was, for the most part, relatively static in space and unchanged by time. When Russian mathematician Alexander Friedman carefully analyzed Einstein's equations of general relativity in the early twentieth century, he found that the universe could not be static according to the theory; it must either be expanding or contracting. For a while Einstein resisted this notion, but later came to accept it as one of the valid predictions of general relativity. And so it was Friedman, according to Ferris, who actually proposed this absolutely revolutionary theme to the scientific community (2).

Observational evidence that accorded with the Bible's centuries-old statements regarding the expansion of the

The Stretched-Out Universe

universe was discovered just over 100 years ago at the Lowell Observatory in Flagstaff, Arizona. Astronomer Vesto Slipher found that of the 40 spiral nebulae that he studied, a surprisingly high 36 showed a shift of their spectra toward longer wavelengths (3). This phenomena, called a redshift, can be taken as evidence for recession from the Earth, much as a lower-pitched whistle tells you that a train is receding from your current position. During the 1920s and 1930s Edwin Hubble and Milton Humeson used new methods of astronomy, including the brightness calibration of a certain class of stars called Cepheid variables, to arrive at the famous redshift-distance relationship known as Hubble's law. This postulates a linear relationship between the speed of recession and distance from the Earth. Additional primary and secondary evidence for expansion has continued to accumulate over the course of the years, including quantitative measurements of the cosmic-background radiation spectra, densities in space of certain types of stars and galaxies as a function of distance, and geometric measurements, among others (4). To top it off, a very surprising discovery has come up in the last ten years or so, which is, that the expansion of the universe is not only continuing but appears to actually be accelerating! According to two cosmologists this is apparently due to some form of "dark energy," with the implication that empty space is full of energy (5).

In explaining the modern scientific view of the universe's expansion, Ferris comments that the notion of an object expanding to fill empty space is not accurate;

rather, space itself is expanding or stretching (6). Note the amazing consistency with the account of Genesis, which tells us that God created the heavens and the earth at the beginning, implying that all of the heavens and the earth were created at that time. Then we are told by the prophet Jeremiah that the Lord "stretched out" the heavens, the same word that modern science uses to describe this phenomenon. There appears to be absolute agreement with the use of such a word as "stretch" in the Bible by the prophets Jeremiah and Isaiah and our modern astronomical models of the universe. Naive notions of stretching might be of stretching the things in space, but not space itself. However, it is this second process that is exactly what the Bible describes and is exactly what is described with our best cosmological models. The absolute accuracy of the Biblical statements truly does point to the one True God of the Bible and the inerrancy of the Biblical account of creation, and thus to the trustworthiness of all of the Bible's words and claims.

22

THE TEMPERATURE OF CREATION

*"From the chamber of the south comes the whirlwind,
And cold from the scattering winds of the north.
By the breath of God ice is given,
And the broad waters are frozen."* (Job 37:9-10)

*"Its rising is from one end of heaven,
and its circuit to the other end;
And there is nothing hidden from its heat."* (Psalm 19:6)

"They need no lamp nor light of the sun, for the Lord God gives them light." (Revelation 22:5)

Yesterday was a hot day in our area. I heard of one mom who remarked, "It's 100 degrees," whereupon her six-year-old son said, "Look on the bright side, it's not 1000 degrees," which puts a rather galactic perspective on our Earthly habitat and, I might add, a fairly good one in my opinion. After all, Venus and Mercury are far too hot for a leisurely summer vacation, and Mars and the rest of the planets in our solar system are far too frigid. Even in temperatures that may be rather uncomfortable for us we seldom reflect on the meaning of the notions of temperature and heat. What is temperature? One physics text tells us that temperature is regarded as a fundamental concept in physics; that is, it cannot be described in simpler physical terms (1). The disciplines of thermodynamics and statistical mechanics inform us that temperature is intimately related to the motion of molecules, and so temperature has something to do with motion and activity at the most basic level. The availability of energy for work is also related to the flow of heat between two physical bodies, and when the potential for this flow is exhausted (and the bodies are at equal temperatures) there can be no more work performed by the system.

The study of the thermodynamic properties of the creation gives us clues as to its history and characteristics. The measured temperature of the universe is now about 2.726 degrees Kelvin (2), but according to what many scientists believe to be a reasonable model for the early universe, an extremely hot and dense creation event occurred in the early first moments of creation (3), with a temperature of ten billion trillion trillion degrees centigrade. Each physical object has a radiation emission spectrum that is related to its temperature. For the universe itself, physicists as early as the 1940s predicted that a background radiation spectrum should be present (4). The current radiation spectrum seems to correspond quite well to a well-known radiative physical model (5). By peering into space at farther and farther distances, and measuring the temperature of molecules using spectroscopy*, cosmologists have found that the farther away they look, the hotter the material is. This is consistent with an object, in this case the entire universe, that is both expanding and cooling down (6).

For those of us who have placed our hope in Christ, although we are in the world, we are not of it. The dangerously high temperature associated with the process of fast oxidation (fire) is sometimes used both metaphorically and literally to represent extreme difficulties of life. The prophet Isaiah says to the Lord's people: "When you walk through the fire, you shall not be burned, Nor shall the flame scorch you" (Isaiah 43:2). The three faithful Hebrew young men in the book of Daniel (chapter 3) experienced this literally when they refused to engage in the commanded idolatry that would have violated their consciences and faith. The Scripture says that King Nebuchadnezzar "commanded that they heat the furnace seven times more

---

* Measurements of radiation as a function of spectral wavelength, which can be used to infer properties of molecules including types and temperature.

than it was usually heated. And he commanded certain mighty men of valor who were in his army to bind Shadrach, Meschach, and Abed-Nego, and cast them into the burning fiery furnace. Then these men were bound in their coats, their trousers, their turbans, and their other garments, and were cast into the midst of the burning fiery furnace. Therefore, because the king's command was urgent, and the furnace exceedingly hot, the flame of the fire killed those men who took up Shadrach, Meshach, and Abed-Nego. And these three men, Shadrach, Meshach, and Abed-Nego, fell down bound into the midst of the burning fiery furnace. Then King Nebuchadnezzar was astonished; and he rose in haste and spoke, saying to his counselors, 'Did we not cast three men bound into the midst of the fire?' They answered and said to the king, 'True O king.' 'Look!' he answered, 'I see four men loose, walking in the midst of the fire; and they are not hurt, and the form of the fourth is like the Son of God.'" (Daniel 3:20-25) And later "they saw these men on whose bodies the fire had no power; the hair of their head was not singed nor were their garments affected, and the smell of the fire was not on them." (Daniel 3:27)

All processes of this universe are impermanent, and scientists who are in the business of making predictions into the distant future billions of years from now predict a time when the last star will burn out (7), temperatures in space will equalize, and there will be no more energy available for work in the universe. Of course, we as Christians hold to the belief, as revealed in the

Bible, that the end will come long before the natural decay and terminal cooling predicted by cosmological physics. It is not that the extrapolations based on the laws of physics are necessarily incorrect from a strictly naturalistic point of view; it is that our faith and the Scriptures inform us of a different end at the return of Jesus Christ, as revealed for example in Peter's second epistle:

"But the day of the Lord will come as a thief in the night, in which the heavens will pass away with a great noise, and the elements will melt with fervent heat; both the earth and the works that are in it will be burned up. Therefore, since all these things will be dissolved, what manner of persons ought you to be in holy conduct and godliness, looking for and hastening the coming of the day of God, because of which the heavens will be dissolved, being on fire, and the elements will melt with fervent heat?" (2 Peter 3:10-12)

23

THE CONSTANTS OF CREATION

"While the earth remains, seedtime and harvest,
Cold and heat, winter and summer,
And day and night shall not cease." (Genesis 8:22)

"Thus says the Lord, who gives the sun for a light by day,
The ordinances of the moon and the stars for a light by
night,
Who disturbs the sea, and its waves roar
(The Lord of hosts is His name):
'If those ordinances depart from before Me, says the Lord,
Then the seed of Israel shall also cease

From being a nation before Me forever.'"
(Jeremiah 31:35-36)

"'Yes, I have loved you with an everlasting love;'"
(Jeremiah 31:3)

"'For assuredly, I say to you, till heaven and earth pass away, one jot or one tittle will by no means pass from the law till all is fulfilled.'" (Matthew 5:18)

"Every good gift and every perfect gift is from above, and comes down from the Father of lights, with whom there is no variation or shadow of turning." (James 1:17)

There are books (e.g. see (1)) that describe how various inventions of man work. Such books are filled with all kinds of interesting details on the workings of basic machines such as inclined planes and pulleys, to quite complicated contraptions such as sewing machines. For many of these machines there are a number of parameters of design that interact and are set to precisely those values that make the mechanism do whatever its designer intended. The grand piano, for instance, has a series of wires, each stretched over a precise distance and tuned to a precise harmonic frequency. The number of wires, their lengths and their harmonics are three of the parameters of the "system," and there are others also. This is so that a large audience can thrill to the music of Mozart as interpreted by a master pianist. The current world of physics has an analogy to these sets of parameters. Ferris remarks regarding the standard model of particle physics that the theory works wonderfully to predict the observations of particle physics but requires a number of ad hoc[*] parametric constituents for which there is no scientific rationale governing their particular values (2). Scientists refer to these numbers as fundamental constants or simply constants.[**]

Constants are to be found in all areas of physics. The special theory of relativity assumes that the speed of light is constant in a vacuum (3)[***]. The masses of the electron, proton, neutron and the other elementary particles, the force strengths of gravity, electromagnetism, and the strong and weak nuclear forces are familiar examples of entities that have constant numbers associated with them. A characteristic of our current understanding of creation is that there are a number of physical constants in the universe which appear to be just so. That is, they have particular values, but the reasons for those values are not currently explainable by any deeper theory. Superstring or M-theory are current attempts that are delving into the matter of a unified theory which if found could explain the reasons for these specific constants (4). Research on a "Theory of Everything" attempts to address this unification issue---but in a broader sense, even if this quest

---

[*] Something apparently necessary but not justified by any deeper theory.

[**] Note that not all constants of physics are "fundamental," as some can be derived from others.

[***] The speed of light is about three times ten to the eighth meters per second in a vacuum.

is successful it would only push the problem to another deeper level, but not remove the "why" question of the particularity of nature's constants. We discuss the precision and precariousness of these constants in other chapters; suffice to say that they are beautifully assigned to just the values required for human life and continued existence. For those who believe that science explains everything, we are still lacking the empirical evidence to support a "scientific reason" for why the constants of nature are so perfectly and precisely assigned. References to a "multiverse" or an infinite number of universes with the implication that ours is just here by chance are currently in vogue among some cosmologists, but the question is raised whether such allusions are in principle not falsifiable and hence not scientific answers at all. Although these supra-physical theories are beliefs of scientists, they are not necessarily scientific beliefs, and there is a big difference between the two. Perhaps science is in principle incapable of addressing the "why" question, as essentially it is not a scientific question after all, and the most that science can do is point out that there is something to be explained here.

There are current discussions as to whether the constants of nature are truly constant and changeless over the time frame of the universe. Astronomers observe distant (both in time and space) objects and try to infer the physical properties of the universe over its history. Based on these measurements, the constants of nature seem to have remained, at the very least, quite close to their current measured values for some time. As for the future, we are told in the book of Hebrews, speaking of the heavens, that "they will be changed, but You are the same, and Your years will not fail" (Hebrews 1:12). The "they" refers to the heavens and the "You" speaks of the Lord, Who truly is forever and does not change. The handiwork and constancy of God's creation is a testament to the Lord's constant faithfulness. We are told that "nor height nor depth, nor any other created thing, shall be able to separate us from the love of God which is in Christ Jesus our Lord" (Romans 8:39). God is truly constantly faithful to His people and He has promised to remain so throughout eternity.

24

REFLECTIONS OF SPLENDOR

*"God came from Teman, The Holy One from Mount Paran.
His glory covered the heavens, And the earth was full of His praise.
His brightness was like the light;
He had rays flashing from His hand..." (Habakkuk 3:3-4)*

*"The people who sat in darkness have seen a great light,
And upon those who sat in the region and shadow of death
Light has dawned." (Matthew 4:16)*

The Character of Creation

"For you were once darkness, but now you are light in the Lord. Walk as children of light..." (Ephesians 5:8)

The process of seeing something depends on light which in some way proceeds from the object. In general, the light may be emitted, reflected, absorbed or transmitted. The green leaves we see have pigments that reflect "green" light strongly, and thus appear as a particular color to our visual system.* The sun emits a tremendous amount of energy in the visible spectrum, and so we are able to see during the day by virtue of reflected light from the sun. The stars also emit their own light, although they appear to be much dimmer than the sun and in fact can only be seen generally without instruments at night. The moon, on the other hand, is cold and does not emit visible light. The light we see from the moon is almost entirely due to reflected light from the sun; in this context both lunar shadows and mountains appear, and three dimensional structure and local surface properties modulate the reflected radiation, giving rise to various observed patterns.

The emission of electromagnetic radiation by matter is an extremely important area of physics. The study of this area led Max Planck to propose a radical new quantized formula for his radiation law, leading to a revolution in physics, and the study of electromagnetic radiation transport and interaction with matter remains

---

* "Green" and other perceived colors are actually made up of a combination of the visible wavelength spectrum.

a productive area of research to this day. Scientists have discovered that electromagnetic (EM) radiation (of which visible light covers a fraction of the spectrum) can be coherent (as with lasers) or incoherent (as with electric light bulbs), and possesses both wave and particle properties.

The practical importance of visible reflections impact us every day of our lives in everything we see, most of the time without our giving the physical mechanisms any thought whatsoever. It turns out that there is a tremendous amount of information contained within the spectral distribution of intensities of light and the broader EM radiation spectrum. The field of remote sensing uses spectral images to help classify land cover, with applications to agriculture, geology, hydrology, archeology, meteorology, navigation, and archeology, among others (1). In medicine doctors use X-rays, which are pictures derived from differential absorption and scattering of radiation by the tissue within our bodies, to "see" the different body structures such as bones. EM radiation fills the universe and can thus be used to provide information about the farthest observable reaches of space.

The apostle Paul draws an analogy to reflected light in order to describe our experience with God in 2 Corinthians: "But we all, with unveiled face, beholding as in a mirror the glory of the Lord, are being transformed into the same image from glory to glory, just as by the Spirit of the Lord"(2 Corinthians 3:18). The Scripture also says that "God made two great lights: the greater light to rule the day, and the lesser light to rule the night" (Genesis 1:16). Just as the moon does not have its own light, but reflects that of the sun, we also do not have our own glory or shine our own light. Only by "beholding" the revelation of God in Jesus Christ are we "transformed" into the kind of people that God would have us to be. Jesus said, "I am the light of the world" (John 8:12). Our best is when we are reflecting Jesus's glory to a dark world.

25

THE WATERS OF CREATION

"And the Spirit of God was hovering over the face of the waters." (Genesis 1:2)

"Thus God made the firmament, and divided the waters which were under the firmament from the waters which were above the firmament; and it was so." (Genesis 1:7)

"For He draws up drops of water, which distill as rain from the mist,
Which the clouds drop down and pour abundantly on man." (Job 36:27-28)

The Character of Creation

*"By the breath of God ice is given,
And the broad waters are frozen.
Also with moisture He saturates the thick clouds;
He scatters His bright clouds." (Job 37:10-11)*

*"The waters harden like stone,
And the surface of the deep is frozen." (Job 38:30)*

*"When He strengthened the fountains of the deep,
When He assigned to the sea its limit,
So that the waters would not transgress His command..."
(Proverbs 8:28-29)*

*"Ho! Everyone who thirsts, come to the waters..."
(Isaiah 55:1)*

"And Jesus said to them, 'I am the bread of life. He who comes to me shall never hunger, and he who believes in Me shall never thirst.'" (John 6:35)

The molecule H_2O, whose constituents of hydrogen and oxygen are known to nearly every schoolchild, is the commonest of Earthly liquids. In our modern plumbed cities one can turn on the faucet and out it pours. It is wasted in vast volumes, flowing in massive amounts from the mountains to the oceans as if worthless, and yet when truly scarce it is the most precious of commodities. It is essential. It can be transcendentally beautiful. It is big business. The majority of the physical mass of the human body is water; biologically speaking, it is the liquid of life.

So ubiquitous and so familiar is this fluid that most people give very little thought as to the natural properties of this remarkable chemical compound.* Despite its commonness, liquid water is not an "average" liquid. The fact of the matter is, as chemical substances go, water is actually quite uncommon. Experts have remarked on the confluence of a number of quite unusual properties that are found in this single substance. Michael Denton discusses the "fitness" of water for carbon-based life as compared with all other liquids (1). The notion of fitness connects and relates the geophysical, physico-chemical and biological realms in terms of suitability for life. For example, water expands when it freezes, a property that it shares with very few other fluids, and which allows viable geologic water cycles between freezing and warmer temperatures. Another anomaly is water's latent heat of evaporation; it takes more heat per gram to turn liquid water into water vapor than any other liquid at normal temperatures (2). This works to the benefit of the Earth's long-term geothermal regularity and also the thermal regulation of plants, animals and humans. Water exists in

---

* Water is most commonly found on Earth as a liquid, but is found in its solid state in expansive areas and is a gaseous component of our atmosphere. These states depend on both temperature and pressure, so that the state of water in outer space is primarily solid.

liquid form on earth over a range of temperatures and pressures that are optimal for the enzymatically driven biological processes within our cells. There is no other fluid that even comes remotely close to water's combination of ideal-for-life qualities including low viscosity, superb solvent properties, electrical conduction capacity, high latent-heat thermal capacity, freezing and boiling points, and high chemical reactivity with moderate acidity, each ideally suited for life (3). Perhaps to most of us these properties of water just seem "natural" and do not appear extraordinary or provoke any particular notice. Possibly this arises precisely from the fact that the chemical and physical attributes of water are so perfect that they don't draw our attention even though we drink and use water every day of our lives.

Although plenteous on Earth, no other planet in the solar system has any open-to-the-atmosphere liquid water to speak of. One of Jupiter's moons, Europa, appears covered with ice but may actually have liquid watery "oceans" beneath it. Ward and Brownlee point out that scientists look for planets with water as a primary enabler of the possibility of planetary life (4). This is why scientists tend to get so excited whenever there seems to be the possibility of water on other planets in the solar system or beyond. Certainly water is a sine qua non of advanced life.

Modern astronomers have differing theories about the origin of Earth's large volume of water. One theory is that much of the water arrived by way of meteorites that crashed into the Earth. The Bible indicates in Genesis 1:7 that there are waters "under the firmament" and "above the firmament." The book of Job inquires probingly as to water's source: "Who cuts a channel for the flooding rain or clears the way for lightning, to bring rain on an uninhabited land, [on] a desert with no human life, to satisfy the parched wasteland and cause the grass to sprout? Does the rain have a father? Who fathered the drops of dew? Whose womb did the ice come from? Who gave birth to the frost of heaven when water becomes as hard as stone, and the surface of the watery depths is frozen?" (Job 38:25-30 (HCSB)).

We see here that the Lord is asking Job if the rain has a father. Clearly the Lord is the Creator of water and is poetically illustrating this fact in Job. The NKJV translates verse 30 from this passage: "The waters harden like stone, and the surface of the deep is frozen" (Job 38:30). In verses 31-33 there is a continued discussion of stellar constellations and the "ordinances of the heavens," so it appears possible that the context of this text includes the realm beyond our Earthly atmosphere. The temperature of the Earth's atmosphere at altitudes even of commercial aircraft is indeed extremely cold, and can be a cause of concern if there are icy conditions. Extending to space, the picture given in Job is completely correct. Scientists now know that the temperature of interstellar space is extremely low and that the water there, of which there is a voluminous amount, actually is frozen. Thus the Biblical references to "the deep" and "the frost of heaven" are amazingly accurate, indicating both that there is water there and that it is frozen water. So the book of Job predated knowledge of modern atmospheric studies and astronomy by several thousand years in this area. For those who question literal Biblical accuracy this is a challenge, as this Scripture passage from Job is quite ancient and also disagrees with other ancient cosmologies. The book of Job's information regarding this could only have come from a heavenly source, from God Himself.

The amount of terrestrial land cover versus water surface has been studied by geologists and observed to be an important factor for animal habitability. Ward and Brownlee speculate on the importance of the relative surface areas of the continents versus the oceans and discuss the possible effects on temperature if the Earth's precise fraction of surface water cover were different than it is (5). Proverbs 8:29 and Psalm 104:9 talk about this and tell us that the Lord put specific limits on the extent of the waters; again we see the marvelous hand of God's providence in the environmental makeup of the Earth.

Water is important and prominent Biblically. The Hebrew word "mayim," translated "waters," is mentioned in the first chapter of Genesis in the second verse---in fact, prior to "Let there be light." The fact that water is a blessing is universally acknowledged. King David wrote: "You visit the earth and water it, You greatly enrich it; The river of God is full of water; You provide their grain, For so You have prepared it. You water its ridges abundantly, You settle its furrows; You make it soft with showers, You bless its growth." (Psalm 65:9-10)

Perhaps the first and foremost felt benefit of water is that it satisfies our thirst. Built into each of us as a part of our nature is a need for water and a sense of deep gratification at its supply. The prophet Isaiah proclaimed in the Old Testament: "Ho! Everyone who thirsts, Come to the waters..." (Isaiah 55:1). But there is more than the natural H_2O water of this world. In the New Testament Christ said: "Whoever drinks of the water that I shall give him will never thirst. But the water that I shall give him will become in him a fountain of water springing up into everlasting life" (John 4:14). It is this water that only Jesus Christ provides that truly satisfies our thirst.

26

THE PARADOXICAL UNIVERSE

*"Trust in the Lord with all your heart,
And lean not on your own understanding;
In all your ways acknowledge Him,
And He shall direct your paths." (Proverbs 3:5-6)*

"The wages of sin is death; but the gift of God is eternal life through Jesus Christ our Lord." (Romans 6:23 (KJV))

"You did not choose Me, but I chose you…" (Christ speaking to the disciples) (John 15:16)

"The just shall live by faith." (Romans 1:17)

Paradoxes apparently are real. The best scientific minds for over a century have developed a theory of the very small that is called quantum mechanics. The tentacles of the theory affect virtually all of physics. Physicists rely on agreement with experiment to ascertain a scientific hypothesis' or theory's correctness, and in this sense all theories are provisional—that is, it would take only one confirmed experimental refutation to torpedo any currently accepted theory of science. In the case of quantum mechanics, according to Penrose there are no such discrepancies with experiment that are currently known (1). This reflects a nearly universally held assessment by physicists of the success of quantum theory in describing the behavior of the physical world. So what's the problem? Basically, it's that quantum mechanics doesn't make sense, and this also is generally acknowledged even by its foremost proponents. For example, there is the photon's pesky dualism between particle-likeness and wave-likeness. This is famously portrayed by the dual-slit experiment (e.g. see (2)). In this experiment if light is given the opportunity to pass through two slits to get to a detector screen, it happily proceeds to do that and when detected shows an interference pattern that is exactly consistent with a wave that passed through both slits. Thomas Young in he 1800s supported a wave model of light based on this evidence, which is actually quite compelling to this day. However, if a small photon detector is cleverly inserted at each slit to measure which slit the light actually went through, it is always observed that if the light passed through at all, it inevitably went through only one of the slits, as if it were a bunch of particles. Again, this is very compelling evidence, but for an alternative picture of light. So apparently, when one is looking for wave properties, light obediently accommodates and appears as a wave, proceeding through all available openings. Then, when inspecting via experiment for particle behavior, the very same light always passes entirely through just one or the other slit (or neither), but never both simultaneously, appearing perfectly particle-like. Physicists try to explain this by a mathematical indeterminacy that awaits a collapse of the wave function, which occurs in a particular way depending on what experiment is being performed to find a given property. The "collapse" to a particular observation is governed by probability amplitudes that are contained in the Schrodinger equation*. The process of collapsing removes indeterminacy and apparently elevates probability to the status of physical law, in that there is no means to know precisely what will happen (e.g. which slit a particular photon will select) prior to the experiment. The implications of the standard "Copenhagen interpretation"**championed by Bohr, Heisenberg and others bothered several prominent twentieth-century physicists including Einstein and Schrodinger. Erwin Schrodinger dramatized the unseemliness of the standard interpretation of quantum theory

---

* The Schrodinger equation describes the wave-like behavior of particles.

** The Copenhagen interpretation embraces the uncertainty in physics and does not explain it in terms of hidden variables or determinacy.

with his example of a simultaneously alive and dead cat inside a box, awaiting an experimenter's observation, and Einstein famously declared that God does not play dice. And this is not all about quantum weirdness. There is the troubling (Einstein called it "spooky" (3)) appearance of non-locality. That is, a measurement in one place will immediately infer a complimentary measurement of an "entangled" species (particle, photon, etc.) at a distant place, no matter how distant, instantaneously. However, for all the aspiring entrepreneurs out there, this property, even though it is observable, is just enough out of our control that it cannot be used to transmit messages (4), and so no new cell phone apps are in the making with the so-called EPR paradox as it is called after Einstein, Podolsky and Rosen.

No matter what one may think of the physicality of probability amplitudes as they relate to actual reality, they are useful and applicable to real-world descriptions of what we see in nature (5). Several work-arounds to the standard Copenhagen interpretation have been put forward, one involving the multiplication of universes at each quantum "collapse," another invoking pilot waves that look ahead and tell the particle/wave where it can go, and yet another invoking consciousness as that which empowers the reduction to observation of alternatives (6,7). The "many universes" concept that there are zillions of other universes popping into existence each picosecond is rather uneconomical to say the least (e.g. see (8)), not to mention the problem that since any instrument will measure only the physics in one universe, the theory is manifestly untestable. One of the alternative theory's relationship to consciousness appears somewhat nonscientific and difficult to define precisely. What if the observer is not paying attention? Will that change the result of an experiment? One would hardly like to think so, as many things happen while one is asleep or driving the car at rush hour. The possibility of pilot waves along with their non-locality may satisfy the wave-particle duality paradox. However, these paradoxes continue to exist, according to at least one expert, in all interpretations of quantum mechanics (9). It appears that the Lord has made the real world more wonderful and mysterious than we can understand with our minds.

The Bible says "'Who has known the mind of the Lord that he may instruct Him?'" (1 Corinthians 2:16). Also the apostles declared of Christ: "Now we are sure that You know all things, and have no need that anyone should question You" (John 16:30). We see in Scripture that Christ has the attribute of all knowledge, which is a proof that He is God, while at the same time being fully man as Isaiah spoke of Him "For unto us a Child is born" (Isaiah 9:6). He is not in any capacity subject to the uncertainties of nature, as He rules nature and He is the One who truly does comprehend it. So when we see that He chose us (John 15:16), we can understand this by faith and acknowledge the truth of God's ways even if we do not and cannot fully comprehend how "all things work together for good to those who love God" (Romans 8:28).

27

THE MAGNIFICENT CREATION

"When I consider Your heavens, the work of Your fingers,
The moon and the stars, which You have ordained,
What is man that You are mindful of him,
And the son of man that You visit him?" (Psalm 8:3-4)

"'And you forget the Lord your Maker,
Who stretched out the heavens
And laid the foundations of the earth...'" (Isaiah 51:13)

"The heavens declare the glory of God;
And the firmament shows His handiwork." (Psalm 19:1)

The Character of Creation

"Remember to magnify His work,
Of which men have sung.
Everyone has seen it;
Man looks on it from afar." (Job 36:24-25)

People at times have objected to the sheer grandeur, size and magnificence of the universe with respect to the Earth and mankind's limited extent, as if this is some kind of argument against the Creator. The reason, they say, is that it is wasteful to have so many galaxies and stars just for man. After all, hasn't science discovered that we are chance inhabitants of an average planet in an average location in the universe, with an average sun, an average galaxy and an average environment? We have been taught to see nothing special here—and therefore it is supposed to seem reasonable to assume that we are the product of a lucky accident. They "forget," as the prophet Isaiah proclaimed, their Maker.

It is no secret to Scripture or Christian theology that the heavens are vast, mysterious, unsearchable and truly magnificent. God even used this as an analogy of His great promise that He would provide descendants to Abraham in Genesis 15:5: "Then He brought him outside and said, 'Look now toward heaven, and count the stars if you are able to number them.'" Astronomers estimate that there are about 100 billion galaxies in the observable universe, and each of these has from several million to a trillion stars in it (1). Needless to say we have not numbered them all and in fact such a task is totally impossible for us.

The universe may appear huge, wasteful and inefficient, but in fact recent cosmological discoveries have shown that the properties of the entire universe appear to be finely tuned for the type of life that exists on Earth (2,3,4). For example, the amount of heavy metals and radioactive elements in the Earth are just right to maintain a protective magnetic field, support plate tectonics, and develop internal geothermal heat. These are necessary for the existence of liquid water, protection of the atmosphere, and proper mixing of natural elements between the soil and the air. The metals, cosmologists believe, were formed not at the big bang but instead inside the early generations of stars, which as the Scripture tells us in Psalm 8, have been "ordained" by God. So according to this view, the magnificence of the sky that we see each night and the vast expanse of the universe that astronomers carefully observe does not reveal a wasteful universe. On the contrary, cosmological data reveal an exquisitely planned and orchestrated creation, with marvelous grandeur, size and scope, that *only* the "God who alone is wise" (1 Timothy 1:17) could have created.

If the universe appears inefficient or wasteful to us, or the Earth appears comparatively insignificant, perhaps this is because we do not see things through the lens of Scripture and God's revelation. The apostle Paul warned Timothy to avoid "contradictions of what is falsely called knowledge" (1 Timothy 6:20). The

Scripture, speaking of Christ, says "that in all things He may have the preeminence" (Colossians. 1:18). The apostle's perspective, instead of seeing waste, is to acknowledge God's supremacy in all things. If we take this attitude, we begin to observe God's tremendous care for mankind, without adopting a presumptuous type of skepticism as regards the greatness of God's ways. After all, doesn't the book of Isaiah tell us that "His understanding is unsearchable" (Isaiah 40:28)? The observation of the universe, its stars, and the sun and the moon, when mixed with a properly directed and instructed faith, is truly uplifting and calls us to raise our eyes to the Lord our True Creator, and to acknowledge His magnificent work.

28

HIS MIGHTY TORRENTIAL RAINS

"The earth is the Lord's, and all its fullness,
The world and all those who dwell therein.
For He has founded it upon the seas,
And established it upon the waters." (Psalm 24:1-2)

"For You formed my inward parts;
You have covered me in my mother's womb.
I will praise You, for I am fearfully and wonderfully made;
Marvelous are Your works, and that my soul knows very well.
My frame was not hidden from You,
When I was made in secret,

And skillfully wrought in the lowest parts of the earth.
Your eyes saw my substance, being yet unformed.
And in Your book they all were written,
The days fashioned for me,
When as yet there were none of them." (Psalm 139:13-16)

In the wild frontiers of the world of science there is a hot debate between those who contend that the processes of chance mutation and natural selection are indeed adequate to explain the full complexity of life, and those who hold that an intelligent causation for at least some of this complexity and diversity is a better theory, or at least that intelligent causation ought not to be categorically excluded. This is not the first time that a dispute of this type has occurred; nor is the debate between intelligent design and naturalism new, as it transcends several centuries. For those impartial enough to see it, this is an example of the process of scientific turmoil that is described in Thomas Kuhn's classic book, *The Structure of Scientific Revolutions* (1). As discussed by Wells (2), the current dispute bears some familiar earmarks of "normal" scientific revolutions, including a dispute over what constitutes the nature of science and the definition of a particular area of science, the manifestation of divisive camps, a fight between theoretic paradigms, and advocacy for change from those who are not the current insiders.

Part of the dispute arises over what ought to be treated differently when studying one-time origination events versus ongoing processes. Geisler discusses these differences and makes the point that ongoing natural processes and functions cannot provide adequate explanations of origins within nature (3). He divides science into the study of origins and the study of the continual operations within nature. Once this crucial difference is apprehended it is possible to see where both limited microevolutionary processes coupled with intelligent causation and design in biology makes sense, and that these are both compatible within a dichotomous origins-operations framework. The microevolutionary processes may be responsible for some limited modifications of species within Biblical "types" but cannot explain their origins or the actual source of a multitude of significant biological cellular and microcellular structures and their associated information. This is precisely where Behe's formulation of irreducable complexity as a scientific paradigm points to non-naturalistic origins (4), and Dembski's design filter can be used to properly infer design as a cause (5). What doesn't make any evidentiary sense, but what is nonetheless taught almost as a religious mandate in the public schools and universities, is that design must be excluded as a necessary precondition to a theory of origins. This has resulted in a theoretical facade (macroevolutionary theory as creator) that tries to shoehorn an ill-fitting philosophy onto the history of origins of biological events. This approach is an attempt to ignore the real evidence of design in nature, such as the immense complexity of even the earliest and simplest known life, much like the scientists and theologians of Galileo's day who refused to look through his telescope for fear of upsetting their preconceived view of the heavens.

Speaking of the heavens, the dichotomy between origin science and operation science is also to be seen in the realm of cosmology. The study of the universe can tell us a lot about normal physical processes and laws that function both now and in the past. The cosmic microwave background and a number of other evidences seem to provide strong overall evidence that an origin/creation event occurred*. However, the study of the current and past universe can take us only so far. One physicist explains that a common view of the big bang is that it explains the origin of the universe, but that it actually does no such thing; rather, it describes what the universe did a very, very small moment after its origin but doesn't actually account for the origin itself (6). The true explanation for this miraculous event comes from the book of Genesis, of course, where we are told that "In the beginning God created the heavens and the earth" (Gen. 1:1). Faith informs us, based on the integrity of God's word, that there is actually no conflict between the scientific study of the heavens and the Scriptural revelation of "the history of the heavens and the earth when they were created, in the day that the Lord God made the earth and the heavens" (Gen. 2:4). Especially in the last 100 or so years, the statements of the Bible such as the fact that

---

* The author subscribes to the reasonableness of the big bang cosmological model as a physical description of the immediate aftermath of the Biblical creation event.

there was an actual beginning to space and time (i.e. they are not infinite into the past), and the expansion of the heavens, have been confirmed and not contradicted by scientific measurements.

The Bible points to the creation as evidence for God's power, as for example in Jeremiah 27:5: "By My great strength and outstretched arm, I made the earth, and the people, and the animals on the face of the earth" (HCSB). The book of Jeremiah also declares that "He has made the earth by His power, He has established the world by His wisdom, and has stretched out the heavens at His discretion" (Jer. 10:12). To deny the creation as a supernatural event is to deny that God has actually done what He says He has done. People often do this with the mistaken notion that science provides something to back them up; it doesn't. There is no scientific evidence that contradicts divine creation ex nihilo. Thus the distinction between origins and normal operation in science is vital for the Christian so as not to enter into what Dembski describes as an idolatrous form of naturalism that presumes to explain everything and do everything (7). Naturalism as a predominant philosophy is currently in vogue in the courts and secular universities of the land. It is at odds with the doctrine of God as the Creator and Upholder of creation and attempts to include everything under its purview (8). As an example of the naturalistic worldview, there are people who look at the creation and take it essentially as a "mechanical universe." Since the days of Isaac Newton this view has gained popularity, and it is accepted to a certain extent by both orthodox Christians and atheists alike. Christians, however, would reject that the mechanical universe view is able to explain origins of the universe, Earth, our solar system, the sun, the stars, the special attributes of our own planet, or biological creation. It is interesting to note that Newton himself did not completely hold to the mechanical view as regards to origins, but instead considered that the orbits of the planets must have had some help from God to get started and to maintain their motions (9). Newton is considered to be perhaps the greatest scientist of all time; yet if to be scientific today one must adhere to absolute naturalism, then according to the modern revisionist-naturalistic definition of science he may not even be considered a scientist at all!

In chapter one I discussed the view that there are laws that are in operation in the universe, and that physical processes are governed by and act according to these laws. However, to assert that only these laws are in operation, and that only these laws have ever been in operation, and that they were not themselves a product of the Creator's word, is not in itself a scientific statement of fact, but is in reality a proposition of faith in naturalism. But contrary to this assertion there seems to be quite strong evidence that the laws were both extremely finely tuned for our existence, and that some circumstances of creation were set up, quite extraordinarily, in humanity's favor (10). Exclusive naturalism is a more simplistic and crippled philosophy of nature than that which incorporates design. To admit the possibility of design in the universe and nature presents the scientist, theologian and any thoughtful person with the challenge of correctly discerning which phenomena are due to primary nonnatural causes and which are due to natural causes. However, this is no excuse and provides no reason for not being willing to do the hard work of investigation within a framework of scientific empiricism that lets the evidence lead where it may. In perhaps the vast majority of instances the position of attributing events to natural causes will be the proper scientific conclusion. This is especially so in "operations science" that deals with events occurring after an origination event. However, it is no proof of strict naturalism that a vast majority of ongoing events can be entirely ascribed to natural law or contingency. The one-time, non-repeatable activity that is associated with origins events is more difficult to study than ongoing processes, and may not be accessible to the standard empirical hypothesize-and-test methods of science. One must be careful in these cases that there are no hidden naturalistic-only assumptions that render the conclusions invalid. Dembski's design filter (11) would seem to be quite useful in these sorts of tests, with the requirement that nonnatural causes be admitted as a possibility a priori, which is perhaps the key element that exclusively atheistic and naturalistic versions of science omit.

The writer of the book of Hebrews states: "By faith we understand that the worlds were framed by the word of God, so that the things which are seen were not made of things which are visible" (Heb. 11:3). So Bible-believing Christians believe this "framing" occurred, indicating God's work in nature from the very beginning. Regarding God's subsequent hand upon His creation, the premise of God's continued interactions with nature for His purposes are a theme of Job chapter 37. We are told in Job that God continues to work within and upon the realm of nature, with causes that are beyond our limited abilities to measure or ascertain. Speaking of the Lord's works, the author of the book of Job writes: "He saturates clouds with moisture; He scatters His lightning through them. They swirl about, turning round and round at His direction, accomplishing everything He commands them over the surface of the inhabited world. He causes this to happen for punishment, for His land, or for His faithful love" (Job 37:11-13 (HCSB)). And the Scripture adds: "God thunders marvelously with His voice; He does great things that we cannot comprehend. For He says to the snow, 'Fall to the earth,' and the torrential rains, His mighty torrential rains, serve as His signature to all mankind, so that all men may know His work" (Job 37:5-7 (HCSB)).

29

ENTROPY AND THE ARROW OF TIME

"Martha said to Him, 'I know that he will rise again in the resurrection at the last day.'" (John 11:24)

"So the man of God said, 'Where did it fall?' And he showed him the place. So he cut off a stick, and threw it in there; and he made the iron float. Therefore he said, 'Pick it up for yourself.' So he reached out his hand and took it." (2 Kings 6:6-7)

*"He stirs up the sea with His power,
And by His understanding He breaks up the storm."*
(Job 26:12)

*"What man can live and not see death?
Can he deliver his life from the power of the grave?"*
(Psalm 89:48)

Our common sense, developed since earliest childhood, tells us that coffee does not jump back into the cup, once spilled, or that people who have jumped into a swimming pool aren't likely to reverse the process and fly up out of the water completely dry, with the splash simultaneously reversing itself, as all the little drops of water reassemble and magically merge back into the once more smooth pool. None of these things happen as a matter of course. This type of intuitive understanding of how the world works has been fortified for each of us by innumerable observations, and seems compellingly true based on common sense. However, if there is one lesson that 20th and 21st century physics has taught us, it is that common sense derived from everyday experience may not always be a proper guide to the workings of the world, especially in some areas such as the very small, the very massive or the very fast. And our common sense is certainly not a guide to what is possible with God, as the story of Elisha and the ax head quoted previously illustrates.

The examples of the unspilled drink and the backward splash cited above would seem to require time to go "backwards." If one examines the equations of physics that govern motion, they actually are symmetrical with respect to time (1). This may lead one to conclude, simply based on the equations themselves, that the odd phenomena described above might actually occur. So why doesn't a spilled drink jump back into its cup? In a discussion of this issue, Penrose relates the asymmetry of physical processes over time to the laws of thermodynamics; in particular, the second law of thermodynamics (2). Apparently, our commonsensical notion of the behavior of the world, and the general perception of the forward flow of time, are both related to the extremely low entropy of the original state of the universe. The physical argument seems to be that the low entropy[*] (relatively speaking) of the world around us, and the large degree of structure and organization in the universe, is a consequence of the universe's original extremely low entropy at the time of creation. Processes that increase entropy are those that we observe as time moves forward.

To carry this insight further, Penrose calculates the odds of the original low entropic state of the universe (3). This probability turns out to be so low as to be virtually impossible to have occurred randomly. You are more likely, it would appear, to see your spilled coffee jump back into its cup many, many times in a row than to have had the actual highly ordered original state of the universe. The precise universe that we live in, that

---

[*] Low entropy is associated in general with high order.

both believers and nonbelievers live in, that we woke up in this morning, that is physically real, is so improbable from a naturalistic point of view as to be impossible to explain without recourse to an Exceedingly Wise Creator with the power to organize to a level far beyond our comprehension. In light of this knowledge, to assert we are here by chance has an element of irrationality about it. The highly rational alternative to believing that we are here by chance is to have faith in the Creator, whose organizational resources are limitless. Thus, even our common sense, it would appear, is the result of a very "uncommon" aspect of Creation. Perhaps this is one more reason to not trust our own reasoning, but as the Scripture says, to "Trust in the Lord with all your heart, and lean not on your own understanding" (Proverbs 3:5).

30

THE SUSTAINED CREATION

"In the beginning was the Word, and the Word was with God, and the Word was God. He was in the beginning with God. All things were made through Him, and without Him nothing was made that was made." (John 1:1-3)

"...because by Him everything was created, in heaven and on earth, the visible and the invisible, whether thrones or dominions or rulers or authorities—all things have been created through Him and for Him. He is before all things, and by Him all things hold together."
(Colossians 1:16-17 (HCSB))

"'I am the Alpha and the Omega, the Beginning and the End,' says the Lord, 'who is and who was and who is to come, the Almighty.'" (Revelation 1:8)

"'I, Jesus, have sent My angel to testify to you these things in the churches. I am the Root and the Offspring of David, the Bright and Morning Star.'" (Revelation 22:16)

The Lord Jesus upholds the creation even as you are reading this line. The creation came into existence as a response to the Word of God. The Bible tells us that "In the beginning was the Word, and the Word was with God, and the Word was God" (John 1:1). We find Scriptural proof that Christ, the Word, is God in John 1:14 where the Scripture declares "The Word was made flesh and dwelt among us." Later in the book of Revelation the glorified Christ is revealed as the "the Alpha and Omega, the First and the Last" (Revelation 1:11). The revelation of creation as being dependent upon Christ's upholding power is seen in the New Testament book of Colossians verse quoted above. Therefore the creation is neither self-sufficient nor self-existent, and the Bible refutes all new-age notions that elevate earth above the status of a creation under God.

Later in the New Testament we are told by the apostle Peter that "the heavens and the earth which are now preserved by the same word, are reserved for fire until the day of judgment and perdition of ungodly men" and then "the heavens will pass away with a great noise, and the elements will melt with fervent heat; both the earth and the works that are in it will be burned up" (2 Peter 3:7, 10). Thus the sustaining power of God has a time scale that is in God's hand, not ours. The Bible also teaches that our very lives are in the God's hand. King Belshazzar in the book of Daniel made a grave error in judgment by misusing the articles of the temple. The prophet Daniel informed the king: "...the God who holds your breath in His hand and owns all your ways, you have not glorified" (Daniel 5:23). Needless to say, things did not go well for Belshazzar that night.

Let us not make Belshazzar's error in not glorifying the One to whom we owe our lives and by whom our lives consist. As Christians, we can have the confidence in life that Paul declared in Romans 8:31-32 and 8:38-39: "If God is for us, who can be against us? He who did not spare His own Son, but delivered Him up for us all, how shall He not with Him also freely give us all things?. . .For I am persuaded that neither death nor life, nor angels nor principalities nor powers, nor things present nor things to come, nor height nor depth, nor any other created thing, shall be able to separate us from the love of God which is in Christ Jesus our Lord." We trust that Christ's supremacy over this world extends to all circumstances and aspects of both physical and spiritual reality to guarantee ultimate victory for His chosen ones.

31

LINE UPON LINE

*"Your eyes saw my substance, being yet unformed.
And in Your book they were all written, The days fashioned for me,
When as yet there were none of them.
How precious also are Your thoughts to me, O God!
How great is the sum of them! If I should count them, they would be more in number than the sand;
When I awake, I am still with You." (Psalm 139:16-18)*

*"For precept must be upon precept,
precept upon precept,*

*Line upon line, line upon line,
Here a little, there a little." (Isaiah 28:10)*

"For the law was given through Moses, but grace and truth came through Jesus Christ." (John 1:17)

"Therefore the law was our tutor to bring us to Christ, that we might be justified by faith. But after faith has come, we are no longer under a tutor." (Galatians 3:24-25)

Upon the maturing of the physical sciences in the 19th and 20th centuries, it became apparent that a single theory did not fit across all time, energy, size, mass, mass density and velocity scales of physics. Even assuming there is the possibility of one single theory of everything (although it is yet to be discovered), there seem to be strata of current theories that fit well to particular regimes of physical phenomena, and that do not fit or are not useful in other strata. This is true in many different areas of science (1). These "layered" theories may not seem intuitively clear to us unless we have delved into unfamiliar realms of observation and theory, assisted with sensitive observational instruments, where we actually cross into another so-called "level" of modeling and measurement. For example, it is well known that the laws of classical mechanics work well, in fact nearly perfectly, for things like hockey pucks, billiard balls, refrigerators and steam engines. However, they fail miserably when compared to actual experiments at the "very small" or quantum level. At these miniscule dimensions, masses and energies one requires the laws of quantum mechanics to describe the phenomena. The same is true of gravity, for which Newton's theory works fabulously well until one enters the realms of the very massive or very fast, for which general relativity is required. Interestingly, these theories are not just esoteric niceties; we see the actual effects of quantum mechanics every day with the use of microcircuits that include zillions of transistors, each operating according to principles that include essential quantum mechanical properties.

Our learning in the sciences has progressed through stages that are related to the structure of the current layering of theories. Mathematical physics was given an impetus by Galileo, progressed with the theoretical contributions of Kepler, and was formalized in terms of general laws of motion by Newton. Both Kepler and Newton's studies encompassed astronomical scales and effects, which are ideal for the study of gravity, and led to classical Newtonian physics. Quantum mechanics and relativity were thrust upon science in the early twentieth century, leading to revisions to Newton's physics that are absolutely fundamental. The laws of physics continue to be applied to a vast number of specific applications to the present day. Some areas require multiple theories applied together. In weather modeling, for example, there are computer models that include physics of gases, but also must take into account multiple levels of thermal interactions of solar heating and geothermal heating, cooling, conduction and convection.

The presence of multiple levels of organization is found in the biological world as well. There are vastly differing physiological levels within animals, plants and people, encompassing multiple levels of order in terms of structure, size and function. We find enormously complex chemical structures that encode the instructions for development. At the basic information level there are instructions stored in DNA that tell each cell how to develop and function. In some way, the interaction of the various systems is orchestrated as a baby develops and grows in the womb. Cells differentiate into skin, nerve tissue, bones, blood, lungs, kidneys, liver, stomach, and all of our other internal organs and tissues. The organs themselves compose systems of functionality such as the nervous system, respiratory system, immune system, skeletal system, circulatory system, etc. Our understanding of the functionality of the nervous system including the brain is not commonly expressed in the language of the coded DNA. Additionally, the sequence of information that is encoded in the DNA, and its mechanisms for expression in the cells, does not in general tell us how the body functions at the system level (e.g. how you digest your food or perceive music, etc.).

In mathematics and engineering there are very familiar methods of analysis based on what are known as Fourier transformations that decompose signals into multiple frequency components. These components are usually ordered in terms of their resolution, be it temporal, spatial or some other dimension, so that the lower resolution or broader terms come first, followed by the higher frequency terms. The first few coefficients can give enough information to provide a fairly crude representation of a signal (think of a blurry picture as an example), whereas the later coefficients fill in the detail. In the mathematics of Fourier transformation, enough of the frequency coefficients must be present and be measured to get a clear depiction of whatever is being observed. This is analogous to many areas of science and engineering, and is particularly observed in biology and physiology, where theories and parameters over multiple scales may be quite different, and a complete understanding mandates different avenues of research and theoretical levels.

The progression of God's plan for His redeemed has also been revealed in stages. Stephen, in Acts 7 of the New Testament, presents a brief history of God's interaction with His people, proceeding through His appearance and promises to Abraham, Joseph's life, God's faithfulness during the trials of the Israelites in Egypt, the ministries of Moses and David, and the culmination of the prophecies of the "Just One" (Christ) in the coming of Jesus Christ. The apostle Paul in his great epistle to the Galatians tells us that the purpose of the law was to bring us "to Christ, that we might be justified by faith"(Gal. 3:24). Also, writing to the church, in 1 Corinthians the apostle points to our future destiny: "So it is with the resurrection of the dead: sown in corruption, raised in incorruption; sown in dishonor, raised in glory; sown in weakness, raised in power; sown a natural body, raised a spiritual body. If there is a natural body, there is also a spiritual body. So it is written: The first man Adam became a living being; the last Adam became a life-giving Spirit. However, the spiritual is not first, but the natural; then the spiritual" (1 Corinthians 15:42-46 (HCSB)). So we who trust in Jesus Christ for forgiveness of sins and salvation are established in the promises of God for eternal life now and forever, based on the blessed revelation of God to his people from Genesis to Revelation.

32

WHERE TO LOOK

*"I will lift up mine eyes unto the hills,
from whence cometh my help.
My help cometh from the Lord,
which made heaven and earth."
(Psalm 121:1-2 (KJV))*

*"I pray that the eyes of your heart may be enlightened so
you may know what is the hope of His calling, what are
the glorious riches of His inheritance among the saints, and
what is the immeasurable greatness of His power to us who
believe, according to the working of His vast strength. He*

demonstrated {this power} in the Messiah by raising Him from the dead..." (Ephesians 1:18-20 (HCSB))

When we were in Seward, Alaska, on a family vacation, we saw mountains rising up near the sea. There was still snow on the peaks even though it was during July. In Anchorage there was a beautiful range of mountains visible from our hotel window. These mountains are perhaps accessible to men with the right equipment and perseverance. Yet, there are places in Alaska, in fact a great many places, that are only accessible by air. The "bush pilots" with their small planes provide the lone corridors of civilization to these destinations. These aviators fly over and about these austere and forbidding peaks with a regularity and familiarity of those negotiating the morning commute to work on the local freeway. These stark, icy, lonely ranges of mountains are seemingly beyond the reach of man's dominion. Perhaps the "unto the hills" that the psalmist is referring to carries with it the idea of a help that is beyond that which has any source in man's resources. The hills and high mountains are creations of the Lord, and required massive power to forge. Correspondingly, the help that is hoped for in the Lord is hidden at times as if beyond the hills; it is a help apprehended by faith and not by sight. By looking to the hills, the psalmist is perhaps telling us that the only real help for some situations is truly of divine origin, beyond the possible reach, inventions or strength of man. The psalmist apparently reached a point where that was true in his own life, and we all, sooner or later, reach that point in our lives or vicariously in the lives of someone we love.

There is a realm that mankind has always understood is beyond its natural reach—the heavens. Our best and mightiest in-person explorations have brought us no farther than our own moon—a giant step perhaps compared to man's previous abilities, but not even a baby step in comparison to the vastness of the heavens. We need a Creator that can reach down to us. Thankfully, we are told that "Christ Jesus came into the world to save sinners" (1 Timothy 1:15), so that we also may cry out with the psalmist: "My help cometh from the Lord, which made heaven and earth."

33

THE BIG CREATION

"But who is able to build Him a temple, since heaven and the heaven of heavens cannot contain Him?" (2 Chronicles 2:6)

"Is not God in the height of heaven? And behold the height of the stars, how high they are. And thou sayest, How doth God know? Can he judge through the dark cloud?" (Job 22:12-13 (KJV))

"He counts the number of the stars; He calls them all by name." (Psalm 147:4)

The Character of Creation

*"As far as the east is from the west,
So far has He removed our transgressions from us."
(Psalm 103:12)*

"God that made the world and all things therein, seeing that he is Lord of heaven and earth, dwelleth not in temples made with hands;" (Acts 17:24 (KJV))

I remember as a child seeing the Pacific Ocean and being struck by the fact that it was SO BIG. I couldn't see its end; it appeared an almost incomprehensible vastness of water. However, this was just the Earth's vastness. As we learn about the extent of the heavens through the use of astronomical instruments, we have found that they are almost incomparably larger than the Earth. One might say that a defining characteristic of the heavens is that of just plain old "bigness." This has come as a progressive discovery in science that has occurred over the course of several millenia.

The measurement systems used by astronomers have gone through a number of stages. According to one astronomy source, scientific estimates of the extent of heavenly distances date to Hipparchus of Nicaea, who in 189 BC estimated the distance from the Earth to the moon as about seventy-five Earth radii (1). Not bad. Moving forward to just a few hundred years ago, the invention and progressive improvements of various manners of telescopes allowed observation of distant stars, but the distances to these points and clouds of light were difficult to determine based on direct observation. Use of parallax and geometry allowed early modern astronomers such as Tycho Brahe to track the orbits of the planets. Geometric methods also enabled estimates of the distances to the moon, sun, planets and some stars. However, parallax is only useful for estimating distances to fairly close stars. Use of the relative brightness of stars is a possible aid but may not always be reliable, as observed brightness varies with both distance and the type of star, and also may change if there is intervening space dust. In the nineteenth and twentieth centuries, improved telescopes allowed better and better viewing capability and fueled a growing debate over the nature of the starry clouds far off in the heavens. Heber Curtis thought, correctly, that there were other galaxies in the universe besides ours (2). Vesto Slipher was the first to determine by means of spectrographic measurements that nebulae actually were moving at high velocities with respect to the Earth. Edwin Hubble in the 1920s discerned that the nebulae were actually composed of billions of individual stars (3), and studied the distances to the stars relative to their velocities. The discovery of Cepheid variable stars, which vary in magnitude over a period of time with the period related to absolute brightness levels, provided a new method to estimate distances to those stars. Other operating assumptions such as that the brightest stars in each nebula (or galaxy) are approximately equal in absolute magnitude allowed Hubble and others to approximate distances to the nebulae. In 1929 Hubble published a revolutionary finding that stated that the receding velocity of stars is generally proportional to their distance from Earth, a relationship now known as Hubble's law. We now have exquisitely fine astronomical instruments, such as the Hubble space telescope, that are able to measure stars' brightnesses at high resolution and sensitivity, enabling improved estimates of distances to stars and galaxies, and detecting galaxies that are at huge distances from our planet.

The scientific discoveries of astronomy inform us today that there are vast stretches of space that are populated by billions of galaxies, each with billions of stars in them. The most distant of these are apparently billions of light years from Earth, a distance that is virtually impossible to fathom. To get an idea of the magnitude of this length, consider that light travels fast enough to circle the Earth over seven times in one second. There are about 31,556,736 seconds in each year, with one thousand million years in a billion years, and the size of the universe apparently exceeds 10 billion light years. Multiplying these out gives an idea of the huge distances that the universe spans, but does not even measure the full extent of the universe, as there are unseen areas too far to be observed. It is a humbling thing to realize how really small we are compared to the vastness of the universe. This quality of "bigness" may come as no surprise to students of the Bible. There are a number of places in Scripture that refer to it, such as Isaiah 44:24 when it says: "'I am the Lord, who makes all things, Who stretches out the heavens all alone...'"

Thus the size of the universe reminds us that a much greater Creator is responsible for the world, and that we neither control it or even truly comprehend it. Anytime we are tempted to think that we are masters of our own fate, we need only remember that not all the stars have even been discovered by man, although the Bible states in Psalm 147:4 that the Lord has both counted and named them. The Scripture in Romans 1:20 makes quite a remarkable statement regarding the observation of the creation, and relates this to our ultimate accountability to God. It states: "For since the creation of the world His invisible attributes are clearly seen, being understood by the things that are made, even His eternal power and Godhead, so that they are without excuse..."

There is a transcendent message to such a magnificently huge creation. The bigness of creation shouts out a resounding testimony to the grandeur of the Creator's own power, love, understanding and bigness. There is great purpose and wonderfulness suggested by such grandeur. Jesus in Luke 21:28 said there would be a time to "look up and lift up your heads, because your redemption draws near." Even with the most sophisticated sensing instruments, we cannot see to the end of space. The act of looking "up" as an analogy to the physical, is actually a spiritual act of faith. In looking "up" as Christ said, we are looking beyond this world and beyond this creation. The real expectation is for Christ's redemption from beyond the extent of this world or the universe. So we may infer that as meaningful as the drama of human life and death is, and the purposes and plans of this world are, the eternal purpose comes from beyond this universe, as Christ said, "You are from beneath; I am from above" (John 8:23). We may be comforted and inspired that the God who made such a grand and large universe for us to dwell in has also ordained a grand and wonderful plan for His people, and we who are believers in Christ are partakers in His most excellent plan of salvation by faith in Jesus Christ. Someday the Bible says that the "Son of Man" (Jesus Christ Himself) "will send His angels, and gather together His elect from the four winds, and from the farthest part of earth to the farthest part of heaven" (Mark 13:27). We trust that it will be no problem for His angels to perform such a gathering, as Christ, the Lord of all, has ordained it.

34

THE EXTENT OF THE UNIVERSE

"The sky separated like a scroll being rolled up..."
(Revelation 6:14 (HCSB))

"For thus says the High and Lofty One Who inhabits eternity, whose name is Holy: 'I dwell in the high and holy place, with him who has a contrite and humble spirit, to revive the spirit of the humble, and to revive the heart of the contrite ones.'"
(Isaiah 57:15)

*"Indeed heaven and the highest heavens belong to the Lord your God,
also the earth with all that is in it." (Deuteronomy 10:14)*

*"Before the mountains were brought forth,
Or ever You had formed the earth and the world,
Even from everlasting to everlasting,
You are God." (Psalm 90:2)*

According to the theory of general relativity, the universe is, in the words of physicist Max Born, "finite yet unbounded" (1). An analogy that physicists use to help understand this is that the dimensions of space are like the surface of a sphere, which is finite in area and yet has no boundaries. According to relativistic cosmology, space has more dimensions than the surface of a beach ball, but maintains the similar geometric properties of finite dimensions and volume with no boundaries. I personally cannot mentally picture this although I think I generally understand the analogy to the beach ball. There actually exists physical evidence of a fairly straightforward nature that points to the fact that space with its stars as we see them is actually finite, and, perhaps to your surprise, you have already observed this evidence many times. It is simply, as described in (2), that if an infinite number of stars were to exist in infinite space, then the night sky should be bright and not dark. This argument, which is known as Olber's paradox, is the result of an easy calculation that has been known since the nineteenth century. It implies that the universe is therefore limited in either its extent or number of stars, or both. Within the big bang model, the notion of an unlimited spatial extent in all dimensions is not apparently supported by modern cosmology.

Results in mathematical physics that agree with experimental observations may involve integrals to infinity or sums of an infinite number of terms. For example, the familiar "Gaussian" or bell-shaped curve that every statistics student has seen has an area that is finite. This curve occurs in modeling of random processes that are observed in the real world, and is extensively utilized in probability and information theory. The "tails" or sides of the curve go to infinity in both directions and so to calculate the area using integral calculus one must integrate from negative infinity to positive infinity. Whether mathematical physics actually implies the existence of real, infinite, observable physical quantities or dimensions is an interesting question. Indeed, the observation of anything that is truly infinite in this universe is difficult to imagine.

The grandness of the universe is used by the Lord to illustrate the absolute completeness of our salvation in Christ. The Scripture states: "As far as the east is from the west, so far has He removed our transgressions from us" (Psalm 103:12).

Since there is apparently no edge to the universe, based on the surface of the sphere analogy, the distance between "east" and "west" would appear to be a physically undefinable distance. It can never be reached or even approached. We who are in Jesus Christ and are saved can never be joined back to our old sins. Christ has separated them from us by a distance that can never be covered.

35

THE CREATED CREATION

*"For thus says the Lord, Who created the heavens,
Who is God, Who formed the earth and made it..."
(Isaiah 45:18)*

*"It is He that has made us, and not we ourselves,..."
(Psalm 100:3)*

*"For by Him all things were created that are in heaven and
that are on earth, visible and invisible..." (Colossians 1:16)*

"Great is our Lord, and of great power: his understanding is infinite." (Psalm 147:5 (KJV))

*"For this is what the Lord says--
God is the Creator of the heavens." (Isaiah 45:18 (HCSB))*

"I am the Alpha and the Omega, the First and the Last, the Beginning and the End." (Revelation 22:13 (HCSB))

Atheistic doctrines that try to avoid the need for a Creator have tried to attribute self-existence to the universe. A preponderance of cosmological evidence over the past approximately 100 years has made this position increasingly untenable, even from a purely scientific perspective. Evidence from cosmology in no way contradicts, and in many ways supports the fact of creation (1). We often hear these days the story that we and the universe have arrived here by "chance." Some have argued for this by ascribing an almost magical quality to quantum mechanics as a creative force. Dr. R. C. Sproul points out that while chance is a perfectly legitimate and useful concept to explain phenomena in science and engineering, it is not a "thing" with the power to create (2). Quantum mechanics does allow the spontaneous and apparently random appearance of virtual elementary particles, and this happens constantly according to the theory. However, this still does not explain the existence of the universe from true "nothingness." The appearance of virtual particles in quantum mechanics requires the "vacuum," which is not at all the same as nothing. The quantum-mechanical vacuum requires the operation and precise governance of the laws of quantum mechanics and nature, which themselves are not nothing. In fact, they have particular physical properties, which "nothing," by its very definition, does not possess. So, the quantum mechanics-based argument for creation explains nothing in regards to actual origins, and only manages at best to push the question of how the universe began to another physical level. There is no incompatibility with Biblical revelation in this regard; from a Biblical perspective a range of physical models are available as long as they actually do include a supernatural beginning and a creation-ex-nihilo type of event*.

The big bang model, which is our best current physical theory of the development of the cosmos, entails the conclusion that the physical universe and time itself had a beginning (3). Einstein's famous equation $E=mc^2$ relates energy and mass to each other, and nobody in the modern world doubts the fact that this type of exchange happens. However, in all of our scientific advance, we have never "created" as much as one single electron from "nothing." The known laws of physics would have to be violated for the universe itself to somehow "create" any matter-energy on its own. The first law of thermodynamics states that matter-energy

---

* Creation ex nihilo refers to the Christian doctrine that God created the world from nothing.

can neither be created nor destroyed. It is clear that both mass and energy do exist, and so there needs to be a Source of the mass and energy that is above the observable laws of physics and that controls them. The second law of thermodynamics is also problematic for a self-existent and eternal (into the past) universe. Essentially, the second law of thermodynamics states that the disorder in the universe will increase over time. Physical evidence pointing to the universe as a created entity is that, as discussed by Penrose (4), there is no physical explanation for the extremely low entropy (high order) of the initial universe. There simply is no physical law to explain the fantastic amount of order present at creation when all matter, energy and space itself began. In fact the amount of order at the moment of creation was, according to Penrose (5), extraordinarily high, and with no physical explanation for this, a nonphysical Source of order exterior to the "bang" is required to impart the received order into the universe at a finite time in the past. While unexplainable by physics, this order is reasonably and rationally explained by the Scripture's assertion that God "laid the foundations of the earth" (Psalm 104:5). and that "his understanding is infinite" (Psalm 147:5 (KJV)).

We have noted that the big bang theory is the currently best accepted physical model of the origin of the universe. This theory says that the universe started at a point of a singularity that is not explained by the laws of physics. The singularity appears to be a unique beginning to both space and time, at which point the laws of physics break down. Noted astronomer Dr. Allan Sandage, winner of the 1991 Crafoord prize for his fundamental discoveries in extragalactic astronomy, has come out on the side of God being the best explanation for the universe's existence (6). Christians have known by faith for a long time that the world had a definite beginning,* long before the arrival of the big bang model, and continue to be assured of it by Scripture. A number of Christian scientists and philosophers have discussed this issue in recent years and point out that the big bang model and Genesis 1 are entirely compatible (7). But the fact that science offers no firm contradictions to the doctrine of creation as presented in the Bible, and that science cannot explain creation without reference to either unproven or unprovable magical theories, may be an encouragement to those who trust in the veracity of God's word in Scripture, especially when presented with supposedly "scientific" explanations for our existence that tend to leave God out of the equation. Without God there is no equation. Any scientist who claims that science has disproven Biblical creation is really telling you his about his faith, not his science. With respect to the first and second laws of thermodynamics, this author believes that the mass-energy and the imparted order in the universe came directly from the Biblical Creator God and not from any physical origin. This is in accordance with the

---

* St. Augustine and other church fathers discussed the doctrine of creation and explicitly rejected an eternal universe.

"creation ex nihilo" doctrine of creation that is generally accepted by modern orthodox Christians of both the recent and old creation beliefs.

Remember that Jesus said in John 8:58 (HCSB) "I assure you: Before Abraham was, I am," a direct claim of divinity and in particular a clear contradiction to any temporal or physical limits upon His power or Person as the Son of God. Jesus Christ, the eternal Word of God, being Himself God, is not subject to the laws of thermodynamics. He is the One "for whom and through whom all things exist" (Hebrews 2:10 (HCSB)). He said of Himself: "I am the Alpha and the Omega, the First and the Last, the Beginning and the End" (Revelation 22:13 (HCSB)).

36

THE HEAVENS FOR HEIGHT

*"For as the heavens are higher than the earth,
So are My ways higher than your ways,
And My thoughts than your thoughts." (Isaiah 55:9)*

"But who is able to build a temple for Him, since even heaven and the highest heaven cannot contain Him?" (2 Chronicles 2:6 (HCSB))

*"Lord, Your faithful love {reaches} to heaven,
Your faithfulness to the skies." (Psalm 36:5 (HCSB))*

The Character of Creation

*"His going forth is from the end of the heaven,
and his circuit unto the ends of it:
and there is nothing hid from the heat thereof."
(Psalm 19:6 (KJV))*

"I know a man in Christ who fourteen years ago—whether in the body I do not know, or whether out of the body I do not know, God knows—such a one was caught up to the third heaven." (2 Corinthians 12:2)

"For thus saith the high and lofty One that inhabiteth eternity, whose name is Holy; I dwell in the high and holy place, with him also that is of a contrite and humble spirit, to revive the spirit of the humble, and to revive the heart of the contrite ones." (Isaiah 57:15 (KJV))

The human mind/brain combination is able to do mathematics, compose music and understand theology. Beethoven's Fifth Symphony and the theory of quantum mechanics are products of man's genius. Mathematicians have shown that there are twenty-eight fundamentally different ways of doing calculus on a seven-dimensional sphere (1). I am not sure what that means and probably won't ever completely understand it since I find I have enough of a challenge understanding the little bit of calculus that I am familiar with. In spite of the fact that our mind/brains are truly amazing creations of God, it is obvious that they are limited in many ways. One limitation relates to our ability to distribute our

The Heavens for Height

focus of attention. Apparently, concentration on one thing makes most of us less able to "multitask," or give significant attention to other things at the same time. Chess grandmasters can play multiple games at once against less skilled opponents, but even they will probably have their limits against enough good players. The limits of man's cognitive ability shows up in the area of theoretical physics; brilliant theoreticians still need to focus and devote tremendous energies to their field, and even then progress comes in stages and is usually not without difficulty. Einstein is known to have had a few false starts before he finally got on the right track in developing his theory of general relativity. This in no way demeans his achievement; to the contrary, it emphasizes what a difficult and tremendous achievement it actually was. Physicists have developed remarkably accurate theories that describe what actually is observed in experiments; however, the equations at the boundaries of physics still have theoretical issues that the best minds are grappling with as you read this. Coupled with these theories are the ever increasing challenges of observation where, for example, finer and finer resolution and sensitivity is sought in many areas of science. Interestingly, both better astronomical resolution and sensitivity are related to measuring cosmic phenomena at farther and farther distances, and are thereby related to the size (or "height") of the universe (2).

The height of the heavens above the earth is used by the prophet Isaiah as an analogy to the disparity between the Lord's ways and thoughts and those of mankind (Isaiah 55:9). So, we might ask, how high are the heavens? What is God saying to us with this analogy? Astronomers tend to measure the size of the observable universe in terms of the time that light takes to travel, and many believe that a current size of about 13.7 billion light years of the observable universe is correct, based on the physical evidence (3). The distance we call a light year is the distance that light travels in one year, and is, at least to my mind, an almost inconceivable distance. A distance of 13.7 billion light years is truly immense (implying a valid use of the term "astronomical"), and most likely will be forever unreachable in terms of any human transport or communication technology, wormholes notwithstanding*. Even beyond that, it is interesting to note that while we have invented fantastic telescopic instruments that can "see" into the remotest parts of the observable universe, astronomers believe there are some "parts" or "times" of the universe that are presently unobservable and will always remain so. Thus there appear to be "heights" of the physical universe, so to speak, that we can never see into or reach, and we may never know absolutely and precisely the true size of the universe (5). Our understanding of the universe is therefore limited in principle, and we need only observe the night sky to help us develop an appropriately humble attitude

---

* According to astronomer Hugh Ross, wormhole travel would destroy any object entering the wormhole by stretching it into a stream of particles extending for miles (4).

towards the Almighty. In keeping with the Scripture in Isaiah, we should never think that we can understand the full ways of God or His thoughts; in fact, anything that we do understand of God has been revealed to us by Him. Let us remember that if even "heaven and the highest heaven cannot contain Him" (2 Chronicles 2:6 (HCSB)), then the enormously large creation is absurdly minuscule compared to God Himself. And how wonderful it is that Christ, through whom the world was created, would enter our world and become our Lord and Savior. Thankfully, He came down to us; we could never have approached Him otherwise.

37

THE SEPARATE CREATION

*"In the beginning God created the heavens and the earth."
(Genesis 1:1)*

"And he said, Go forth, and stand upon the mount before the Lord. And, behold, the Lord passed by, and a great and strong wind rent the mountains, and brake in pieces the rocks before the Lord; but the Lord was not in the wind: and after the wind an earthquake; but the Lord was not in the earthquake:" (1 Kings 19:11 (KJV))

"He was in the world, and the world was made through Him, and the world did not know Him." (John 1:10)

"And He said to them, 'You are from beneath; I am from above. You are of this world; I am not of this world.'" (John 8:23)

"'I came forth from the Father and have come into the world. Again, I leave the world and go to the Father.'" (John 16:28)

"'Heaven and earth will pass away, but My words will by no means pass away.'" (Jesus, quoted in Luke 21:33)

We are taught by Biblical Scripture that the world is not God, is not a part of God, and is not divine (1). Such is the false doctrine of the pantheists and New Agers, but such beliefs are not Biblical. The Biblical Scripture teaches us that the world is a creation of God that was formed to be inhabited, as the book of Isaiah (Isaiah 45:18) informs us. We find no place in Scripture that tells us that the earth is alive or is the source of life (God is). Neither is the creation spoken of in Scripture in the dualistic sense of early gnosticism, where good is equivalent to spirit and what is evil or fallen is equivalent to material or physical. In Genesis chapter one (Gen. 1:31), Moses concludes with the summary statement "Then God saw everything that He had made, and indeed it was very good." This statement apparently referred to the entirety of the physical creation. This is also indicated in the book of Colossians which, speaking of Christ, says: "For by Him all things were created that are in heaven and that are on earth, visible and invisible, whether thrones or dominions or principalities or powers. All things were created through Him and for Him." (Col. 1:16) Thus the creation is neither divine nor intrinsically evil.

As things that are neither living nor divine, the Earth and universe are not owed any spiritual worship whatsoever. This may offend many today whose sensibilities have been hypnotized with the modern mind-set of the Earth as something to be honored or worshipped. We are directed by God to steward the Earth, but not to honor or worship it or participate in any system of religion that does. The character of the creation is such that this is not appropriate, and is in truth a form of idolatry.

On the other hand, the Scripture encourages us to study God's handiwork in creation. Study of the creation points to God's attributes, as stated in the book of Romans: "For since the creation of the world His invisible attributes are clearly seen, being understood by the things that are made, even His eternal power and Godhead, so that they are without excuse..." (Rom. 1:20). One of the attributes of God that is brought to light by this Scripture is God's "eternal power." In contrast, the heavens and the earth shall "vanish away," as stated by the prophet Isaiah (Isaiah 51:6). Thus the creation, the universe and the Earth cannot actually be a part of God who is eternal. Neither are matter or energy existent without God, as the pure naturalists assert.

There is a hope in the realization that this world is not the all in all. Christ encouraged us along these lines with His promise in John's gospel: "'Let not your heart be troubled; you believe in God, believe also in Me. In My Father's house are many mansions; if it were not so, I would have told you. I go to prepare a place for you. And if I go and prepare a place for you, I will come again and receive you to Myself; that where I am, there you may be also. And where I go you know, and the way you know.'" (John 14:1-4) One verse later Jesus removes all confusion about the "way" not being of this world or part of this world. In perhaps one of the simplest, clearest and most direct Biblical claims of Christ as the only Savior, Jesus says, speaking of Himself: "I am the way, the truth, and the life. No one comes to the Father except through me." (John 14:6)

38

THE GOODNESS OF CREATION

"Then God saw everything that He had made, and indeed it was very good." (Genesis 1:31)

"Our help is in the name of the Lord, the Maker of heaven and earth." (Psalm 124:8 (HCSB))

"'And My people shall be satisfied with My goodness,' says the Lord." (Jeremiah 31:14)

The Character of Creation

"Or do you despise the riches of His goodness, forbearance, and longsuffering, not knowing that the goodness of God leads you to repentance?" (Romans 2:4)

In the first book of the Bible God pronounced His creation *"tob,"* or good. Goodness seems to be something that, in my experience, most people intrinsically want even though they may not know where to find it. It encompasses love, purpose and value. One dictionary definition of "good" has to do with adhering to a moral basis that is in the universe (1). Thus we may infer that the creation in its original state was not morally corrupt. The word "good" also has another definition that implies its connection with economic satisfaction (2). From these definitions we infer that the goodness pronounced on the creation was in relation to the creation's usefulness for God's purposes in it and for it. It was not random, useless, purposeless, or morally defective. It was purposeful, sufficient for physical need, and beneficial for man.

For Adam and Eve, even before there was written Scripture, there was the visible creation to testify to the goodness of God. They found themselves living in a garden that the "Lord God" had Himself planted (Genesis 2:8). And the Garden of Eden was apparently quite a great place to live. Genesis 2:9 states that "the Lord God made every tree grow that is pleasant to the sight and good for food. The tree of life was also in the midst of the garden, and the tree of the knowledge of good and evil."

The Goodness of Creation

So we see that while the environment was supportive and comfortable, the garden was also an arena that included themes of both divine purpose and spiritual testing. And the blessings of their surroundings continuously testified of the power and goodness of the Lord God as Creator. It is interesting that it was not God's power that the serpent called into question during that first encounter with the first couple. The account in Genesis (chapter 3) relates the events: "Now the serpent was more cunning than any beast of the field which the Lord God had made. And he said to the woman, 'Has God indeed said, "You shall not eat of every tree of the garden"?' And the woman said to the serpent, 'We may eat the fruit of the trees of the garden; but of the fruit of the tree which is in the midst of the garden, God has said, "You shall not eat it, nor shall you touch it, lest you die."' Then the serpent said to the woman 'You will not surely die. For God knows that in the day you eat of it your eyes will be opened, and you will be like God, knowing good and evil.'" (Gen. 3:1-5) We see that the enemy of man's soul maligned God's intentions, using both subtlety and error. Notice that it came down to God's word versus the serpent's word, and one of them had to be wrong. In fact, one of them had to be lying. Initially, it was Eve who was in the position of having to decide which to believe, either the Lord God or the serpent. There was an act, or lack thereof, that would evidence her commitment to either the veracity or falsity of the Creator's word. And her decision would ultimately determine her relationship with God. We might ask what was there to vouch for the integrity of God? It appears that at least one of the witnesses to Adam and Eve on behalf of the Creator's truthfulness and love, and to the integrity of God's word and hence His trustworthiness and goodwill towards His creation, was the goodness of the creation all around them. They had no Bible to read at that time, but they did have the witness of the creation. We are told by the apostle Paul in Romans 1:20 that "His invisible attributes are clearly seen, being understood by the things that are made, even His eternal power and Godhead, so that they are without excuse."

Adam and Eve were blessed with the witness of the creation as it existed prior to the fall. The garden met their every physical need. Their work in the garden gave them purpose, and through it they obtained sustenance. They had fellowship with each other and with the Lord, as evidenced by Genesis 3:8 which indicates that the Lord walked in the garden and visited with them. It appears that there was no lack of provision in the garden whatsoever. All these things should have cried out to them that the entire creation was "very good" as stated in Genesis 1:31. Adam and Eve had blessings all around them to vouch for the love of their Creator for them; yet they also had a test. It seems that faith, fellowship and friendship are always tested. Even though the goodness of God was manifestly apparent to Adam and Eve, the genuineness of the intentions of the Author of such blessings was called into question by the serpent. We too are able to look at that which remains of the goodness of God in creation. It is our choice to acknowledge the blessings of our Creator toward us, or to live in ignorance of His goodness and defiance of His greatness. To be sure, there is much sin and evil and fallenness everywhere, but that should not blind our hearts to the truth behind the creation, and of the ultimate plan of the Lord for those who are His. The Scripture says in Jeremiah 24:6 "For I will set My eyes on them for good..." So the Lord has a good plan for our lives; not our plan, and often not our version of goodness, but a plan based on His goodness.

When the serpent tempted Adam and Eve, there was never a question raised that there was a True Creator. What was in question was what Adam and Eve really believed about the character of the Creator: was He really good, or was he trying to hold back something good from the first humans? If Adam and Eve considered God's goodness as manifested by His creation, then they would also have had strong reason to mistrust the serpent's motives. And when we behold a glorious sunset, a magnificent coral reef, a beautiful forest or the immense grandeur of the night sky, I believe that most people know deep in their hearts that the original design of the creation was good. In the book of Acts the apostle Paul, speaking of the Lord's blessings on mankind, said: "Nevertheless He did not leave Himself without witness, in that He did good, gave us rain from heaven and fruitful seasons, filling our hearts with food and gladness" (Acts 14:17). All these are evidences towards the character of the One who is the Provider and who "gives to all life, breath, and all things" (Acts 17:25). In Scripture we see the wonderful works of Jesus in healing and deliverance from sin. So we, as did Adam and Eve, have a test – what is our response to our Lord's call: "Come to Me, all you who labor and are heavy laden, and I will give you rest. Take My yoke upon you and learn from Me, for I am gentle and lowly in heart, and you will find rest for your souls. For My yoke is easy and My burden is light" (Matthew 11:28-30).

39

THE SEVERITY OF CREATION

"Enter by the narrow gate; for wide is the gate and broad is the way that leads to destruction, and there are many who go in by it." (Matthew 7:13)

"For this they willfully forget: that by the word of God the heavens were of old, and the earth standing out of water and in the water, by which the world that then existed perished, being flooded with water. But the heavens and the earth which are now preserved by the same word, are reserved for fire until the day of judgment and perdition of ungodly men." (2 Peter 3:5-7)

The Character of Creation

"Therefore consider the goodness and severity of God: on those who fell, severity; but toward you, goodness, if you continue in His goodness. Otherwise, you also will be cut off."
(Romans 11:22)

There are places in our world that appear to be about as desolate and barren as possible. While the habitable landscape of the surface of our planet is vast, there are still many fierce and hostile places that we all tend to avoid. Consider the fiery paths of volcanoes, the forbidding peaks of high mountains, or the forsaken furnaces of arid deserts where one would never want to be found. The Earth has beautiful lakes but also frozen glaciers, lovely hills that give way to ominous mountains, gentle waves but also towering tsunamis. Even the earthly locations that are favorable to human life experience occasional severe weather such as hurricanes, droughts, floods, etc., which can cause extreme havoc and which, at least temporarily, make life very challenging or even impossible. In addition to environmental dangers, there are numerous other types of assaults on life's capacity. Biological perils have plagued mankind for millenia, causing pandemics that have brought untold suffering and death. Stupendous advances in medicine and bacteriology such as Fleming's discovery of penicillin have pushed back at the microbe's fury, yet disease and aging inevitably affect each of us. And while the Earth has remarkable protective coverings from solar and galactic radiation as a result of its magnetic field and ozone layer, its protections are imperfect so that from space we are daily exposed to gamma and UV radiation that may be contributing to cell damage, mutations, and reduced life spans (1).

The galaxy is filled with expansive regions that are even more extreme with regard to their unfriendliness to life. Some astronomers have made a case that only small regions of the universe may be able to support advanced life and that most of the entirety of space is hostile to any kind of advanced life (2,3,4). The SETI* crowd is eternally hopeful but thus far have no positive evidence for extraterrestrial life. It is not known how Earth-like any of the so-far discovered extra-solar planets really are, and there is evidence that many of their planetary systems are not amenable to Earth-like planets (5). We are informed in Isaiah 45:18 that the Earth was formed "to be inhabited," but the Biblical Scriptures give no indication that any other place in all of natural creation had such a destiny attached to its origin. The Earth appears to be an oasis in the midst of a galactic desert.

Anyone who is a student of history or who even observes the evening news knows that we live in a fallen world. The Scripture itself tells us that "the creation was subjected to futility" (Romans 8:20) and that the creation "has been groaning together" (Rom. 8:22 (HCSB)). In some way, the subjugation of the created order to a less than perfect status that includes

---

* Search for Extraterrestrial Intelligence

"groaning" is within God's plan for this universe. And this extends to His predestined, elect children in this world. In Christ's narrative of the rich man and Lazarus (see Luke 16:19-31), it was the poor beggar who was covered with miserable sores and who longed for scraps to eat who later inherited eternal life. As for the rich man who was clothed in linen and fared "sumptuously" every day, his eternal fate was the fiery torment of hell. We should not pretend that everything is or should be wonderful here and now (it certainly was not that way for Lazarus), or that the presence of imperfections in this world implies a less than good and saving God. It is vital that our view of God reflect a theology that is not sentimentalized by philosophical notions of a friendly Santa Claus-like god-personage. C.S. Lewis's lion, at once untamed and inscrutable, yet good, is a better metaphor. A view that portrays God as only dispensing blessings, only saying nice and peaceful things to His people and His enemies, and in general only being pleasant, is nowhere to be found in Scripture. We are commanded to consider not just God's goodness, but both the "goodness and severity" of God. This presents a challenge to the modern mind-set that has progressively tried to reduce God to our understanding, and extract properties of God from nature that appear reasonable to our intellectual sensibilities (e.g. see Hunter (6) for an excellent discussion of this trend over last several hundred years). Lost, or at least well hidden in modern popular discourse, are the Biblical doctrines of repentance, judgment to come, punishment for sin, and especially the exhortation to "flee from the wrath to come" (Luke 3:7). Ironically, such distortion of the gospel also eliminates the need for man's redemption and limits the value of the cross of Christ, which is our only means of Spiritual help. As inhabitants of this fallen creation, we find that there are many struggles and much suffering and sorrow. For those who have obtained the grace of salvation through Jesus Christ, there is a wonderful destiny. For God's chosen people there truly is "a future and a hope" as the Bible tells us in Jeremiah (Jer. 29:11). But what of "the severity of God"? Just as there are places of severity in this creation, and places where we would just as well avoid, so there are spiritual places of severe danger, and we are well advised to avoid those paths, for they lead to ultimate destruction. Christ Himself advised us: "Enter by the narrow gate; for wide is the gate and broad is the way that leads to destruction, and there are many who go in by it" (Matthew 7:13). Many today prefer to believe in the existence of heaven, but at the same time discount the warnings of Christ Himself about avoiding the reality of hell. We must consider that He spoke these words not as an idle exhortation, but as an urgent plea regarding the importance of repentance.

40

THE POWER OF CREATION

"Ah, Lord God! Behold, You have made the heavens and the earth by Your great power and outstretched arm. There is nothing too hard for You." (Jeremiah 32:17)

"Jesus answered and said to them, 'You are mistaken, not knowing the Scriptures nor the power of God.' " (Matthew 22:29)

"...concerning His Son Jesus Christ our Lord, who was born of the seed of David according to the flesh, and declared to be

the Son of God with power according to the Spirit of holiness, by the resurrection from the dead." (Romans 1:3-4)

"God, who gives life to the dead and calls those things which do not exist as though they did;" (Romans 4:17)

"For I am not ashamed of the gospel of Christ, for it is the power of God to salvation for everyone who believes, for the Jew first and also for the Greek." (Romans 1:16)

"...and the weakness of God is stronger than men." (1 Corinthians 1:25)

A van that we used to own had a 4.3 liter V6 engine. My wife is the one who mostly drove that vehicle. I'm not sure exactly how much horsepower the van had, but she told me that she could punch the gas pedal and get around anybody. On an everyday basis we relate to different levels of horsepower – for example, how much power it takes to get up to freeway speeds on a steep Sierra mountain highway or for a race car to accelerate out of a curve. There are also progressions of power that are manifested in the universe. Some have been harnessed by man while some are completely untameable. When I fly out of town on a business trip, the engines on the passenger jet are able to lift the multi-ton vehicle off the ground and into the air. And yet the plane remains tied to the Earth's gravity all the while we are in flight. The

Saturn rockets that powered the astronauts to the moon developed a huge amount of thrust as they propelled the enormous vehicle to escape velocity from Earth, and yet this could only be maintained for a short while. We have seen the energy of the atom split by man's invention and are awestruck at the unleashing of such a huge amount of energy; however, this is multiplied millions of times every second in the sun. Astronomers have measured the energy of supernova* events that are as bright for a short period as millions of suns, and yet this still is minuscule in comparison to the total energy in the universe.

The immensity of the power of creation is virtually incomprehensible to us. There are approximately 100 billion galaxies, each with perhaps billions of stars. (Our own Milky Way galaxy has approximately 200 billion stars.) The credit for creation that the prophet Jeremiah assigns to the Lord is associated with the statement "There is nothing too hard for You" (Jer. 32:17). This brings honest observers to realize that mankind, in all its modern technical wizardry, can do absolutely nothing comparable to the Lord's power in creation and that there are many things that are, and always will be, too hard for man. The Scripture declares in the book of Romans: "For since the creation of the world His invisible attributes are clearly seen, being understood by the things that are made, even His eternal power and Godhead, so that

---

* Supernova are extremely powerful and destructive explosions that occur at the final stage of the existence of some stars.

they are without excuse" (Romans 1:20). The creation points to the power of the Creator in such a way as to unambiguously denote His eternal power – the power to create, maintain, order, and also to terminate the universe. Added to all this, it is God's power alone that gives and sustains life (John 1:2-3).

In the gospel Christ told us about the power to be manifested at the end of the age at His return. He states: "Immediately after the tribulation of those days the sun will be darkened, and the moon will not give its light; the stars will fall from heaven, and the powers of the heavens will be shaken. Then the sign of the Son of Man will appear in heaven, and then all the tribes of the earth will mourn, and they will see the Son of Man coming on the clouds of heaven with power and great glory. And He will send His angels with a great sound of a trumpet, and they will gather together His elect from the four winds, from one end of heaven to the other" (Matthew 24:29-31). The fact that the "powers of the heavens will be shaken" would seem to indicate that God's manifest power at the end of the world will overrule all the power of this present order of creation. We are told of some of the Old Testament saints that "were tortured, not accepting deliverance; that they might obtain a better resurrection" (Hebrews 11:35 (KJV)). For the Christian this aspect of the gospel of Jesus Christ is good news, for our home is not this world or this creation, as wonderful and amazing as this creation is. We look to God's resurrection power in Jesus Christ and the power of Christ's return. Amen!

41

THE CREATION INSPIRES

*"When I consider Your heavens, the work of Your fingers,
The moon and the stars, which You have ordained,
What is man that You are mindful of him,
And the son of man that You visit him?" (Psalm 8:3-4)*

*"For You formed my inward parts; You covered me in my mother's womb.
I will praise You, for I am fearfully and wonderfully made;
Marvelous are Your works,
And that my soul knows very well." (Psalm 139:13-14)*

*"O Lord, our Lord,
How excellent is Your name in all the earth!" (Psalm 8:9)*

After a number of revolutions of the moon, the crew of Apollo 8 took turns reading verses from the book of Genesis to a live television audience on the Earth over two hundred thousand miles away. The huge Saturn V rocket and its inhabitants had escaped the Earth's gravitational hold and taken a historic leap into space, and an acknowledgment of God as the Creator of all was entirely appropriate. They apparently did not have the attitude of the group of people in Genesis who, in attempting to build the tower of Babel, sought their own praise and forgot the God who created the heavens. God invites us to give Him acknowledgment and praise for His superiority over us. In the book of Job, the Almighty counsels His servant thus: "Can you bind the cluster of the Pleiades, Or loose the belt of Orion? Can you bring out Mazzaroth in its season? Or can you guide the Great Bear with its cubs? Do you know the ordinances of the heavens? Can you set their dominion over the earth?" (Job 38:31-33)

The creation, when considered for its vastness, for its power, for its depth, for its structure, for its ordinances, and for its beauty and elegance, ought to inspire a sense of praise for the Creator. The great Johann Kepler was apparently extremely moved by his studies of astronomy, writing: "I may say with truth that whenever I consider in my thoughts the beautiful order, how one thing issues out of and is derived from another, then it is as though I had read a divine text, written into the world itself, not with letters but rather with essential objects, saying: Man, stretch thy reason hither, so that thou mayest comprehend these things" (1). Those of us whose surroundings consist of the edifices of civilization with towering high-rises and concrete boulevards, live in a world of electric glow that often diminishes our ability to appreciate the majesty of God's creation. During the day, instead of trees and forests and lakes we see buildings and freeways, and at night, instead of the starry heavens declaring the glory of God to us, we are surrounded by the artificial shine of strip malls and street signs. However, the stars are still there, as is the Lord who created them. Praise the Lord!

42

THE SECRETIVE CREATION

*"As you do not know what is the way of the wind,
Or how the bones grow in the womb of her who is with child,
So you do not know the works of God who makes
everything."*
(Ecclesiastes 11:5)

*"It is the glory of God to conceal a thing: but the honor of
kings is to search out a matter." (Proverbs 25:2 (KJV))*

"'He who reveals secrets has made known to you what will be.'"
(Daniel 2:29)

"The significance and joy in my science comes in those occasional moments of discovering something new and saying to myself, 'So that's how God did it.'"
Henry F. Schaefer (1)

The history of science shows us that whenever we think we have nature finally figured out, that is the time to watch out. Nature often seems to always have another trick hidden up its sleeve. One example from the world of physics occurred during the late nineteenth century when the successes of Newtonian physics and Maxwell's equations seemed to suggest that there were no more fundamental advances required. One story has a famous physicist advising a young scientist to enter a different field, as the only remaining tasks in physics were to extend the decimal places of physical constants by additional significant digits. It was on the heels of this sentiment that the entire world of physics was overturned with the dual developments of quantum mechanics and relativity, both of which revolutionized classical physics. Another example had to do with entrenched beliefs about the infinite and static nature of the universe. During the first part of the twentieth century astronomical measurements evidencing an expanding universe indicated that the universe is indeed neither infinite nor static, which were the prevailing scientific views, but has limits in time and space. This was theoretically indicated also by Friedman in his analysis of Einstein's equations of general relativity. Another case illustrating the phenomena of discovery of previously unknown and unexpected facts is drawn from the area of mathematics, where Kurt Godel showed in the 1930s that there are mathematical statements that cannot be reached by logic and a set of axioms; they are unreachable, perhaps temporarily, perhaps always.

Isaac Newton is famously quoted as saying, "I do not know what I may appear to the world, but to myself I seem to have been only like a boy playing on the seashore, and diverting myself in now and then finding a smoother pebble or a prettier shell than ordinary, whilst the great ocean of truth lay all undiscovered before me" (2). Sometimes surprises come washing up all unexpected onto the shore of observation. A famous quip by quantum physicist I. Rabi at the measurement of the apparently unwanted and unneeded muon* was "Who ordered that?" (3). Sometimes the sand on the seashore of creation is there for all to see, but requires a different perspective. Such was the case with Max Planck who in an "act of desperation" adopted a quantized model of radiative emission, thus forever transforming our understanding of physics (4). Every physicist knew of the problem with classical

---

* A short-lived elementary particle that has some similarity to an electron, but with a mass that is over two hundred times as large.

theory in describing the observed radiation-emission spectra as a function of wavelength, but it was Planck who finally proposed the correct solution by adopting a totally revolutionary concept. Similarly Edison, while working towards a goal of the possibility of an electric light, had to stubbornly ignore those who publicly judged the idea to be absurd, and continued to persevere with his vision (5).

The origin of life is a matter that is of keen exploratory interest to Christians and nonbelievers alike. At its root the answer to this question speaks to our own identity and purpose for existence. A number of theories have been proposed ranging from self-catalyzing RNA to crystals to unknown clay-based reactions to deepwater, self-sustaining chemical reactions. Although there continue to be hopeful naturalistic theories, no scientist can give a naturalistic explanation for life's origin based on solid evidence. For example, there is no geophysical evidence that the type of so-called chemical "soup" postulated by Oparin and relied upon by both replicator-first and metabolism-first models ever existed outside of a test tube. Actual chemical pathways that are supposed to lend evidence to the existence of the early prebiotic compounds have been demonstrated in the laboratory, such as the famous Miller-Urey experiment that generated certain amino acids from ammonia, methane, hydrogen gas and water, but, critically, no oxygen, which would have prevented the desired reaction. However, there is now evidence that molecular oxygen was present in the early atmosphere, thus eliminating the Miller-Urey hypothesis from legitimate consideration (6). Other chemical pathways to key ingredients that are hypothesized to be critical to prebiotic evolution have also been found in the laboratory, but are also considered infeasible in the early Earth environment (7).

As pointed out by Dembski and Wells, there is also no evidence that any form of life simpler than a prokaryotic* type of cell ever existed at any time in Earth's history (8), which is somewhat analogous to saying that no machine simpler than a moon rocket ever existed prior to the rocket. Thus, naturalistic theories of life's origin all have tremendous obstacles to face in explaining the actual information in even the simplest living cell. As an alternative hypothesis, Dr. Stephen Meyer proposes a better argument in which the secrets of creation point to its Source, and draws an inference to a Designer of life's information based on the actual evidence of design in the cell, due to its extremely high information content and the observation that all known sources of information are the result of intelligent beings (9).

One of the age-long secrets of the universe that continues to be investigated by scientists has to to with its origin. Investigation continues because, at whatever point we are in a scientific process, we still do not have all the details. It is well to consider that whatever our current scientific view of the origin of the universe is, we are at best only partially correct—and this is not to

---

* Organisms such as bacteria are prokaryotic; they lack nuclei and their DNA is not arranged in chromosomes.

disparage science or scientists. Rather, it is the nature of science to change over time, and this has been happening at a fairly rapid rate over the last several centuries in regards to scientific theories of astronomy. For example, Copernicus, while stating that the Earth revolved around the sun, also thought that the sun was the center of the universe. Scientists now no longer consider this to be the case, and in fact many do not believe that there is a "center," so to speak, in the traditional sense of the word. Scientific questions about the origin of the universe address issues such as physical models of elemental formation, how old the universe is, and spatial expansion rates and causes, etc. The Biblical Scripture is unchanging and infallible according to the orthodox Christian view**, but is not written in a way that settles all scientific issues. It does, however, speak about some important issues such as (a) the universe had a very definite beginning, (b) the universe is and has been expanding and is not continually contracting, expanding and re-emerging in a kind of infinite cyclical process, (c) the things that we can "see" were not made of the same kind of "visible" things, and (d) there will be a removal of the created things someday by God. The first two of these points separate the Bible, in terms of scientific propositions, from some other major world religions. These clear Biblical claims are in agreement with current scientific theory. Claims (a)

** The author adheres to this view and considers the Biblical Scriptures of both the orthodox Protestant Old and New Testaments to be the only revealed word of God that are infallible.

and (b) are also ones that can be tested scientifically; as stated by astrophysicist George Smoot, "There is no doubt that a parallel exists between the big bang as an event and the Christian notion of creation from nothing" (10). Claims (c) and (d) are theological claims that, to this author's knowledge, science does not speak to. Believers in Christ and the truth of the Biblical revelation trust that they have (as in (c)) and also will (as in (d)) occur as surely as the scientifically testable statements (a) and (b) have occurred.

The things of the kingdom of God are also not obvious at times. Jesus Christ told a parable with a message of His kingdom: "Again, the kingdom of heaven is like treasure hidden in a field, which a man found and hid; and for joy over it he goes and sells all that he has and buys that field" (Matthew 13:44).

Here we find the Lord describing His kingdom as a hidden treasure that is found almost accidentally. The person who realizes what he has stumbled across is then willing to make any sacrifice for the huge riches that it represents. So it is with those who are partakers of "the riches of the glory of this mystery among the Gentiles: which is Christ in you, the hope of glory" (Colossians 1:27). The Lord spoke to Abram, "Do not be afraid, Abram. I am your shield, your exceedingly great reward" (Genesis 15:1) Although some may see only a field and not the treasure hidden beneath the ground, to those who have found Christ as Savior, He is their great riches in this life and the next.

43

THE MATHEMATICAL LANGUAGE OF THE UNIVERSE

"'But you, Daniel, shut up the words, and seal the book until the time of the end; many shall run to and fro, and knowledge shall increase.'" (Daniel 12:4)

"How precious are your thoughts to me, O God! How great is the sum of them!" (Psalm 139:17)

"Great is our Lord, and mighty in power; His understanding is infinite." (Psalm 147:5)

The Character of Creation

"'Now we are sure that You know all things, and have no need that anyone should question You. By this we believe that You came forth from God.'" (John 16:30)

The practice of science entails portraying the world accurately, elegantly and efficiently. Even as English has preempted other languages to become the primary language of common communication in the West, so it is that mathematical language has preempted other linguistic means of representing abstract physical models of the world. Galileo made the point that "Philosophy is written in this grand book of the universe, which stands continually open to our gaze. But the book cannot be understood unless one first learns to comprehend the language and to read the letters in which it is composed. It is written in the language of mathematics..." (1). In reflecting on this, it is really a very remarkable and curious phenomenon that many of the concepts of mathematics, at times developed before the notion of their utility as physical models or without regard to their real-world application, should be suitable for the accurate description of God's creation. Attributing both geometrical mathematics and our ability to comprehend it to God, Johann Kepler wrote "Geometry is unique and eternal, a reflection from the mind of God. That mankind shares in it is because man is an image of God" (2).

The form of thinking and communicating that we characterize as mathematical has, in fact, been one of the key elements that has allowed us to describe the natural world. Science is based on matching observation with theories, and well developed theories, it turns out, are most precisely expressed mathematically. The possibility that a physical concept can also be explained in other languages such as English, Russian, French, German, etc., is almost incidental; the key relationships of a mature physical theory are virtually always expressed either symbolically (e.g. as in chemistry where symbols represent chemical entities) or mathematically, with accompanying text to show the application, purpose, materials, conditions, etc. For a theory in its early development the descriptions are sometimes qualitative, but become quantitative as the theory matures. This extends from the minutest biology to the grandest theories of space, time and matter. Mathematical understanding enables prediction, control and optimization. Jet airplanes would not be flying through the skies each day without mathematical models of structural reliability informing their design specifications. Nor would we be able to go to the optometrist and order lenses that precisely correct our individual vision defects without highly accurate mathematical formulas describing refractive optics. The "reach" of mathematics has become so broad that we take it for granted that any model about the physical world will end up either being written in, or associated with, some manner of mathematics.

Physical mathematical statements tend to be general in form, economically ignoring the many incidentals of the world with condensed relationships that hold broadly. A well-known example of generalization is the equation $V=IR$ describing the relationship between voltage, current, and resistance in electrical circuits. This equation, known as Ohm's law, holds for a virtually infinite number of combinations of V, I and R, and for a vast multitude of different types of wires and resistors. It apparently holds in outer space and a mile under the Earth, and it was just as valid one hundred years ago as it is today. Thus only four symbols elegantly encapsulate many possibilities. Physics is a system that puts a tremendous amount of faith in the structure of mathematical statements about reality. Given I and R, one knows V based on the mathematics of multiplication, and scientists and engineers would not doubt that this law will hold when presented with a new apparatus even if they have not yet tested it.

Scientists tend to assume a priori that mathematics will eventually find its way into any field. As an example of this type of confidence, Newton wrote regarding the study of light: "A naturalist would scarce expect to see the science of [colors] become mathematicall, & yet I dare affirm that there is as much certainty in it as any other part of Opticks" (3). The modern masterpieces of quantum mechanics and relativity theory are essentially mathematical constructs that make statements about what we observe in the real world. These tend to be in the form of generalizations and predictions of what we expect to measure when we look in such and such a way for such and such a phenomenon. Without mathematics there would be no modern theory of gravity expressed as general relativistic equations, nor would there be the quantum mechanical understanding of Heisenberg's uncertainty principle, or precise relationships regarding entropy and enthalpy in physical chemistry, or differential equations governing enzymic rate relationships in biochemistry, or descriptions of the random capture of photons by astronomical instruments, and the list goes on and on.

The fact that some mathematical concepts have worked their way into science may at first seem odd. Complex numbers are required in physics equations that conform to real-world experimental measurements. The mathematics of quantum mechanical amplitudes involves both probability theory and complex numbers. Complex numbers include "imaginary" numbers which, while a standard mathematical concept, are not so easy to imagine, as they involve the square root of negative one. Nevertheless, nature evidently works with interactions that are described by the rules of complex arithmetic, even though our natural intuition built on experience with real numbers is not completely satisfied.

Probability theory is a mature scientific and engineering discipline that, interestingly enough, had its early origins in the analysis of games of chance. Functions related to probability densities and the mathematical rules for calculating the probabilities of random events are needed in describing the behavior of the quantum world. For example, the well-known phenomenon of the diffraction of light is related to quantum mechanical amplitudes at the single photon level, and the probability of decay of an unstable nucleus in any set period of time is well described by a Poisson random variable. Whether or not quantum behavior actually is fundamentally random (which Einstein apparently never accepted but which Bohr viewed as correct), the language of mathematics allows us to understand and model these real-world phenomena. While not being able to predict the outcome of a specific quantum event, we can say what the average expected outcome of a given quantum experiment over many trials will be. These types of statements can be made to be precise and exact using the language of mathematical physics and probability. Without such language this understanding could not exist, and so we see here a rather surprising confluence of the language of mathematics and our best abilities to describe the actions of the real world using mathematical tools that were not originally developed for that purpose.

Thus, the "faith" of scientists in the applicability of mathematics appears to be not without substance. But what is the basis of this belief? It is just that mathematical symbols and language describe and compactly generalize what actually happens, to the extent that we can measure it. In science, this faith must be put to the test by observation, prediction, and experiment (most of the time preceded, if truth be known, by a great deal of speculation on the part of all involved). For example, the famous two-slit experiment has photons behaving one way if both slits are uncovered, and behaving another way if one of the slits has a tiny measuring device on it that tells the experimenter that a photon just passed through that slit. In actual practice, the photons seem to not want to let absolutely precise knowledge of both their position and momentum be known, leading physicists to say things like "the wave function collapses" and to write down equations capturing that collapse. This is fine mathematically, and the structure of quantum mechanics is inseparably tied to the uncertainty principle, as it is called (which, by the way, is itself precisely expressed as a mathematical inequality). However, how a photon at the open slit actually "knows" that there is a detector lurking at one of the slits is still a mystery. All is mathematically reasonable but not "understood" in a way that makes many people feel comfortable with an intuitive mental picture. The mathematics *is* the mental picture.

In summary, the widespread applicability of mathematics in science seems to be based on a fundamental characteristic of the real world; which is, that models that describe the world are best stated mathematically. Why this should be so, it seems to this author, is a profound philosophical question. And while each person can reach the limit of their abilities in mathematics at some level, this is not so of the Creator who designed the mathematical fabric of the stars. It appears that the Creator blended intricate artistry with eloquent mathematics, and has granted us some small ability to comprehend His artistry. We find that there are deep and beautiful mathematical relationships that describe the fundamental physical laws of the universe. The beauty does not contradict the validity of the mathematical patterns just as a sunset is not less beautiful when one understands the principles of refraction of light. We generally tend to regard mathematical insight as a sign of intelligence; thus the mathematical fabric of the universe points in the direction of absolute worship of the Creator who "made the heavens skillfully" (Psalm 136:5 (HSCB)) and whose "understanding is infinite"(Psalm 147:5).

44

TO EVERYTHING A PURPOSE

"And now the Lord says, who formed Me from the womb to be His Servant,
To bring Jacob back to Him, so that Israel is gathered to Him
(For I shall be glorious in the eyes of the Lord, and My God shall be My strength), Indeed He says, 'It is too small a thing that You should be My Servant
To raise up the tribes of Jacob, and to restore the preserved ones of Israel;
I will also give You as a light to the Gentiles,
That You should be My salvation to the ends of the earth.'"
(Isaiah 49:5-6)

The Character of Creation

*"For thus says the Lord, Who created the heavens,
Who is God, Who formed the earth and made it,
Who has established it, Who did not create it in vain,
Who formed it to be inhabited..." (Isaiah 45:18)*

"...who has saved us and called us with a holy calling, not according to our works, but according to His own purpose and grace which was given to us in Christ Jesus before time began..." (2 Timothy 1:9)

*"It is well known that carbon is required to make physicists."
Robert Dicke (1)*

Many modern pop intellectuals would urge us to adopt a sort of "all is vanity" attitude toward life. This is not surprising given a view of life and the universe that excludes the hand of God and the purposes of creation as revealed by Biblical Scripture. The implications of this type of thinking are often not stated in so many words, but they reveal a purposelessness to life that is absolutely unfulfilling. One observes grand edifices of arguments such as Darwinism, existentialism, and the new atheism, all foundationless towers built on sand and ultimately destined to be blown away. What is so remarkable about this is that claims of meaning-without-creation come from some of the most intelligent and best scientific thinkers of our society. Leaders in the judiciary arena, sadly, are also in many cases now aligned with this camp, bequeathing to our society only the transient perspectives of men instead of stable and truly moral laws that accord with the Lord's unchanging moral code revealed to us in the Bible.

Let us examine for a moment the implications of the prevailing worldview of our elite educational institutions. They insist that an atheistic form of Darwinism is true and that we all just happened to gradually get here by chance out of some original chemical goo that just happened to be there as a result of the physical aspects of the universe, which happened to be perfectly suited for life and which also non-miraculously, miraculously appeared. We must believe, and we are told without proof, that all these are without design, guidance or purpose. The pure naturalists then insert that there is an honor and dignity to man because of some self-manufactured qualities. But this is simply untrue if one takes their philosophy at face value. Indeed, there can be no absolute truth or transcendent meaning to life if one truly believes the Darwinist story to be fully factual. When all that remains are the slowly dying embers of the last ancient burned-out stars drifting in cold dark space, then what, we may ask, was our ultimate purpose or dignity if there is no Creator and no absolute truth or higher purpose to life? None, to be sure, in spite of much human grief and suffering, joy, exuberance, plans and perils. Thus the modern diseases of lack of meaning and absence of purpose are the inevitable logical extensions of a system of educational and media indoctrination that relies on no absolute truth and defiantly insists on an ignorance of God's revealed purposes and plans for us.

Scripture plainly tells us that the Earth was created with a purpose, "to be inhabited," as the book of Isaiah tells us. This is strongly supported by our current knowledge of nature. An excellent review into the chemical and biochemical properties of the universe as they relate to life is presented by biologist Michael Denton (2). He documents the point that for quite a broad spectrum of life-related processes there are ideal elements or substances available in nature. As remarkable as this is, he also discusses the fact that for virtually all of the ingredients required for life there are no other chemical substitutes available in nature that even come in a close second in terms of meeting the needs of earthly forms of life. There is no honey to replace sugar in the recipe, no margarine instead of butter, no blue cheese instead of thousand island. As an example of this, if we look at the properties of water as compared to other liquids with respect to life's needs, we find no other suitable substance to bathe and engulf life's multiplicity of processes. Water is perfect for its function as a solute for life-supporting biochemistry, but there would be no close-second substitute solute if water were not here; it's water or nothing in terms of its combined properties of solubility of organic compounds, support for buffering agents, electrolytic properties of materials in solution, heat capacity, and viscosity. Or take carbon. It is the perfect element for the infrastructure of carbohydrates, proteins and nucleic acids, each absolutely critical for life, with again no realistic runner-up element. This repeats again and again in nature over the spectrum of life's needs. It turns out that the materials of the creation, and particularly those present in just the right quantities on Earth, are uniquely suited for the sustenance of life for beings that are basically like ourselves. The essential building blocks of physics and chemistry are observed to be perfectly suited for life. The very ingredients of the universe, it would appear, were meant to allow life, but only by the finest of margins, as if to indicate to observers how amazing and precise this characteristic of creation actually is. Darwinism cannot be the source of the life-supporting properties of nature, as the putative adaptive ability of life depends on these properties and in no way is their origin. Such arguments point in the teleological direction, not in the direction of randomness of nature. Thus nature itself argues for purpose, not just a mechanistic or random structure of events, but actually a higher goal-oriented design imprinted into the fabric of all material creation.

The reality and superiority of God's power in creation lead to the conclusion that our true purpose must be with reference to that which is beyond the universe itself. We are told in 2 Corinthians 4:18 that "the things which are seen are temporal; but the things which are not seen are eternal" (KJV). For the Christian, our purposes are with respect to God's purpose in Christ for mankind. Paul describes this in his glorious letter to the Ephesians: "... just as He chose us in Him before the foundation of the world, that we should be holy and without blame before Him in love, having predestined us to adoption as sons by Jesus Christ to Himself, according to the good pleasure of His will, to the praise of the glory of His grace, by which He made us accepted in the Beloved" (Ephesians 1:4-6).

45

THE INVISIBLE CREATION

"He stretcheth out the north over the empty place, and hangeth the earth upon nothing." (Job 26:7 (KJV))

"'The wind blows where it wishes, and you hear the sound of it, but cannot tell where it comes from and where it goes. So is everyone who is born of the Spirit.' Nicodemus answered and said to Him, 'How can these things be?'" (John 3:8-9)

"For the invisible things of him from the creation of the world are clearly seen, being understood by the things that

are made, even his eternal power and Godhead; so that they are without excuse:" (Romans 1:20 (KJV))

" 'Daughter,' He said to her, 'your faith has made you well.' " (Jesus to a woman, Luke 8:48 (HCSB))

"For we walk by faith, not by sight." (2 Corinthians 5:7)

Ever since the early development of radio waves for communication, the modern world has been inundated by the unseen realities of the electromagnetic spectrum. Television, cell phones, and GPS navigation are all dependent on the transmission of information using invisible electromagnetic radiation. And who has not had the experience of playing with toy magnets, either trying to push two equivalent poles together or pull two opposite poles apart? There is nothing visible between the two positive poles of two bar magnets to keep them apart; yet, they are nearly impossible to force together. There is something quite powerful and very real about these invisible forces of nature. Thus, the falsity of the notion that something needs to be visible in order to be real is directly demonstrated to each of us many times each day.

One of the remarkable realizations that one comes to when studying physics is that there are unseen forces and substances of nature. There is an entire invisible infrastructure, so to speak, that impacts the character of the universe. There are invisible mechanisms by which laws that are observable in their actions on matter and energy operate, the nature of which have been deduced by careful observation of their effects. Isaac Newton described the force of gravity and was aware of its ability to exercise force at a distance, but refused to speculate as to its cause. In his own words, "Gravity must be caused by an agent acting constantly according to certain laws, but whether this agent be material or immaterial I have left to the consideration of my readers" (1). Einstein went on to describe gravity in his theory of general relativity, and yet this extensive force, while apparently intimately tied to the shape of space-time, remains invisible while physically pervasive.

Michael Faraday employed the notion of spatial "fields" related to force relationships of magnetism and electricity. He found that these fields were consistent with his experimental findings of the behavior of electricity and magnetism. These invisible entities played a major role in 19th century classical physics. James Clerk Maxwell wrote down equations precisely describing the electromagnetic force relationships, and Maxwell's equations, as they are known, remain staples in the education of all physics students. Today's physics uses the field concept in characterizing the invisible electromagnetic, gravitational, and strong and weak nuclear forces, and even hypothesizes an all pervasive Higgs energy field*. Mathematical descriptions of the

---

* The Higgs boson is a prediction of the standard model of particle physics that imparts mass to other particles. Recent experimental evidence indicates with high probability that it has now been detected.

properties of these invisible fields have been worked out by theorists, and thus the character of the invisible is both observationally and theoretically manifested; the invisible is real.

One of the most striking and yet to be resolved issues in modern cosmology is that of dark matter. One writer notes that the mystery of dark matter is one of the most problematic issues of modern astronomy (2). The problem is observed at galactic scales, where there doesn't seem to be enough mass to account for apparent gravitational effects. For example, astronomers are able to measure, using spectroscopic methods, the velocities of different areas of observed galaxies. Calculations have been made, based on standard physics, of the motion of the spiral arms of galaxies. However, when observations are compared to these predictions, it turns out that a lot more mass than is directly observed is required to account for the apparent motion. Because scientists are generally reluctant to postulate new laws of physics or even to alter the known laws without highly compelling evidence, the alternative to this is to assume that there is so-called "dark" matter that does not interact with photons in the same way as normal matter. The dark matter would, however, exert gravitational influences similar to all other matter. So, there is a search for what this dark matter material could possibly be, with possibilities ranging from dim matter such as dust that is just very hard to observe, to undiscovered exotic particles.

The Invisible Creation

What do these unseen realities tell us about the true character of creation? The history of radio waves may be instructive. Radio waves cannot be "seen" or "felt" directly, and were not discovered until relatively recently in human history. We now say that there is no mystery to this; we can certainly detect them and know that they are photons[*] within a certain range of wavelengths. Further, we know that they exist even though they cannot be directly seen.

The very small constitutes one realm of physical reality for which there will always be limits on our abilities to directly observe. This has led to indirect methods and inferred models. The concept of a quantized world was rather forced upon physicists. It was a sort of desperate grasp at a description of physical reality using a mathematical construct that only allowed certain energies to exist. The fact that the quantum model precisely fit the experimental results gave physicists insight into the world of electromagnetic radiation and the very small world of photons and elementary particles. Nevertheless there remains a mystery as to what might be thought of as an accurate picture of what really goes on regarding quantum interactions and the ubiquitous wave-particle duality (3). Perhaps we will never be able to form a representative mental image of the most fundamental components and processes of the universe.

---

[*] The photon is the basic unit (discrete quanta) of electromagnetic radiative emission, transmission and absorption.

Nevertheless, quanta and photons and electromagnetic waves are physically real and observable; they do exist and do things. Physical reality is not challenged by our inability to fully picture it. There are "things," such as quantum interactions, the fabric of space-time, and possibly "strings" or other elementary structures that we in principle may never be able to directly observe. There is currently another huge mystery, involving the behavior of the entire universe, regarding what is speculated to involve so-called "dark energy." In contrast to dark matter, dark energy is hypothesized to be an antigravitational force that is causing the universe to accelerate its expansion. This was discovered in the late 1990s and was a complete surprise to cosmologists, who still are in the dark as to the precise nature of dark energy (4). One theory is that it is an energy field called "quintessence" that fills space; another is that it corresponds to Einstein's cosmological constant, and yet another is that gravity itself may be responsible.

We see from everyday life, to standard physics, to the boundaries of cosmology that there is an invisible nature that pervades all of creation. Given this, the Biblical declaration that "The just shall live by faith" (Romans 1:17 (KJV)) is, even for the most empirical among us, an absolutely sensible and rational manner of life. We are told in the Bible that there are "invisible" attributes of God that are discerned from observation of His creation. So we have the truth of Scripture as set forth by the apostle Paul almost two thousand years ago: "For the invisible things of him from the

The Invisible Creation

creation of the world are clearly seen, being understood by the things that are made, even his eternal power and Godhead" (Romans 1:20 (KJV)). Finally, we are told that there is an unseen world that is real and lasting "for what is seen is temporary, but what is unseen is eternal" (2 Corinthians 4:18 (HCSB)).

Notes

Introduction

1. *Merriam Webster's Collegiate Dictionary, 11th edition* (Springfield, MA: Merriam-Webster, Inc., 2005).

2. M. Caspar, *Kepler* (New York: Dover Publications, Inc., 1993).

Chapter 1: The Ordinances of the Heavens

1. I. Newton, "General Scholium of Principia," in *Great Books of the Western World,* ed. R. M. Hutchins, (Chicago: Encyclopedia Britannica, Inc. 1952), vol. 34, p. 369.

2. J. H. Brooke, *Science and Religion: Some Historical Perspectives* (Cambridge: Cambridge University Press, 1991), Ch. 2.

3. J. Strong, *Strong's Exhaustive Concordance of the Bible: with Brief Dictionary of the Hebrew and Greek Words* (Michigan: Baker Publishing Group, 1989).

4. J. H. Brooke, *Science and Religion: Some Historical Perspectives* (Cambridge: Cambridge University Press, 1991), Ch. 1.

5. M. Caspar, *Kepler* (New York: Dover Publications, Inc., 1993).

Chapter 2: Design

1. P. C. W. Davies, *The Accidental Universe* (Cambridge: Cambridge University Press, 1982).

2. F. Crick, *What Mad Pursuit: A Personal View of Science* (New York: Basic Books, 1988).

3. P. Johnson in *The Creation Hypothesis: Scientific Evidence for an Intelligent Designer,* edited by W. A. Dembski (Downers Grove, IL: InterVarsity Press, 1994), Forward.

4. H. L. Poe and J. H. Davis, *Science and Faith: An Evangelical Dialogue* (Nashville, TN: Broadman and Holman Publishers, 2000), Ch. 1.

5. William A. Dembski, *Intelligent Design* (Downers Grove, IL: InterVarsity Press, 1999), Ch. 5.

6. William A. Dembski, *Intelligent Design* (Downers Grove, IL: InterVarsity Press, 1999), Ch. 6.

7. W. A. Dembski and J. Wells, *The Design of Life: Discovering Signs of Intelligence in Biological Systems* (Dallas, TX: The Foundation for Thought and Ethics, Dallas, 2008), Endnotes to Ch. 8, p. 298 of hardcover edition.

8. Roger Penrose, *The Emperor's New Mind* (Oxford: Oxford University Press, 1989), Ch. 7.

9. Hugh Ross, *The Creator and the Cosmos: How the Greatest Scientific Discoveries of the Century Reveal God, Third Edition* (Colorado Springs, CO: Navpress, 2001), Ch. 14-16.

10. J. F. Ashton, Ed., *In Six Days: Why Fifty Scientists Choose to Believe in Creation* (Green Forest, AK: Master Books, 2001), Ch. 24.

11. See note 5 above.

12. See note 6 above.

Chapter 3: God and Gravity

1. E. Hecht, *Physics: Calculus* (Pacific Grove, CA: Brooks/Cole, 1996), p. 239.

2. F. E. Manuel, *A Portrait of Isaac Newton* (New York: D. Capo Press, Inc., 1968).

3. Isaac Newton, "First letter to Richard Bentley (1692)" in *The Works of Richard Bentley, Vol. III,* edited by Alexander Dyce (London: F. Macpherson, 1838).

Chapter 4: Windows of Vision

1. C. S. Lewis, "Is Theology Poetry?" in *The Weight of Glory* (San Francisco, CA: Harper San Francisco, 2001).

2. D. Macaulay, *The New Way Things Work* (Boston, MA: Houghton Mifflin Company, 1998), p. 250.

3. G. Gonzalez and J. W. Richards, *The Privileged Planet* (Washington, D.C.: Regnery Publishing, Inc., 2004), Ch. 4.

4. Ibid.

5. G. Gonzalez and J. W. Richards, *The Privileged Planet* (Washington, D.C.: Regnery Publishing, Inc.), 2004.

Chapter 5: The Delicate Balance

1. R. P. Crease and C. C. Mann, *The Second Creation* (New York: Macmillan Publishing Company, 1986), Ch. 7.

2. J. D. Barrow and J. K. Webb, "Inconstant Constants: Do the inner workings of nature change

with time?" *Scientific American Special Addition* (June 26, 2006): pp. 65-71.

3. L. Strobel, *The Case for a Creator* (Grand Rapids, MI: Zondervan, 2004), Ch. 6.

Chapter 7: Precept Upon Precept

1. S. Patterson, "Masters of the Air," *George Fox Journal Online*, vol. 1, no. 3, (Fall 2005).

2. Ibid.

3. William H. Cropper, *Great Physicists* (Oxford University Press, 2001).

4. B. H. Mahan, *University Chemistry* (Reading, MA: Addison-Wesley Publishing Co., Inc., 1965).

5. Roger Penrose, *The Emperor's New Mind* (Oxford: Oxford University Press, 1989), Ch. 6.

6. R. Jastrow, *God and the Astronomers, second edition* (New York & London: W. W. Norton & Company, 1992), p. 105.

Chapter 8: The Unique Creation

1. N. Geisler, *Systematic Theology: God/Creation, Volume two (Minneapolis, MN:* Bethany House, 2003), Ch. 19.

2. William A. Dembski, *Intelligent Design* (Downers Grove, IL: InterVarsity Press, 1999), Ch. 8.

Chapter 9: A Higher View

1. R. Burnham, A. Dyer and J. Kanipe, *Astronomy: The Definitive Guide* (New York: Barnes and Noble Books, 2003).

2. M. Rees, General Editor, *Universe: The Definitive Visual Guide* (London, UK: Dorling Kindersley Limited, 2005).

3. G. Gonzalez and J. W. Richards, *The Privileged Planet* (Washington, D.C.: Regnery Publishing, Inc., 2004), Ch. 11.

4. L. Strobel, *The Case for a Creator* (Grand Rapids, MI: Zondervan, 2004), Ch. 7.

5. See note 3 above.

6. P. D. Ward and D. Brownlee, *Rare Earth: Why Complex Life Is Uncommon in the Universe* (New York: Copernicus/Springer-Verlag, Inc., 2000).

7. Hugh Ross, *The Creator and the Cosmos: How the Greatest Scientific Discoveries of the Century Reveal God, Third Edition* (Colorado Springs, CO: Navpress, 2001), Ch. 14.

Chapter 10: The Skillful Creation

1. L. Strobel, *The Case for a Creator* (Grand Rapids, MI: Zondervan, 2004), Ch. 6.

2. Hugh Ross, *The Creator and the Cosmos: How the Greatest Scientific Discoveries of the Century Reveal God, Third Edition* (Colorado Springs, CO: Navpress, 2001),

Ch. 14.

3. Hugh Ross in *The Creation Hypothesis: Scientific Evidence for an Intelligent Designer,* edited by J. P. Moreland (Downers Grove, IL: InterVarsity Press, 1994), Ch. 4.

4. See note 2 above.

5. See note 2 above.

6. M. Denton, *Nature's Destiny* (New York: The Free Press, 1998), Ch. 6.

7. Ibid.

Chapter 12: The Complexity Chasm

1. Stephen. C. Meyer in *Mere Creation: Science, Faith and Intelligent Design,* (Ed.) W. Dembski, (Downers Grove, IL: InterVarsity Press, 1998), Ch. 5.

2. Michael Denton, *Nature's Destiny* (New York: The Free Press, 1998), Chapter 4.

3. M. Behe, *The Edge of Evolution* (New York: Free Press, 2007), Ch. 8.

4. William A. Dembski, *Intelligent Design* (Downers Grove, IL: InterVarsity Press, 1999), Ch. 6.

5. W. Dembski, *Intelligent Design* (Downers Grove, IL: InterVarsity Press, 1999).

Chapter 13: The Aging Creation

1. B. H. Mahan, *University Chemistry* (Reading, MA: Addison-Wesley Publishing Co., Inc., 1965).

2. G. Gonzalez and J. W. Richards, *The Privileged Planet* (Washington, D.C.: Regnery Publishing, Inc., 2004), Ch 7.

3. F. Bueche, *Introduction to Physics for Scientists and Engineers* (New York: McGraw-Hill, 1969), Ch. 17.

4. A. Hayward, *Creation and Evolution* (Minneapolis, MN: Bethany House Publishers, 1985), Ch. 7.

5. See note 1 above.

Chapter 14: The Conservative Creation

1. W. A. Dembski and J. Wells, *The Design of Life: Discovering Signs of Intelligence in Biological Systems* (Dallas, TX: The Foundation for Thought and Ethics, 2008).

2. Ibid.

3. P. A. Nelson in *Mere Creation: Science, Faith and Intelligent Design,* edited by W. A. Dembski (Downers Grove, IL: InterVarsity Press, 1998), Ch. 6.

4. M. Denton, *Nature's Destiny* (New York: The Free Press, 1998), Ch. 4.

5. F. Rana, *The Cell's Design: How Chemistry Reveals the Creator's Artistry* (Grand Rapids, MI: Baker Books, 2008), Ch. 11.

Chapter 15: The Dust of Creation

1. M. Denton, *Nature's Destiny* (New York: The Free Press, 1998).

2. Ibid.

3. Ibid.

4. J. D. Barrow and J. K. Webb, "Inconstant Constants: Do the inner workings of nature change with time?" *Scientific American Special Addition* (June 26, 2006): pp. 65-71.

Chapter 16: The Rational Universe

1. *Merriam-Webster's Collegiate Dictionary 11th Ed.*, (Springfield, MA: Merriam-Webster, Inc., 2005)

2. William A. Dembski, *Intelligent Design* (Downers Grove, IL: InterVarsity Press, 1999).

3. Max Caspar, *Kepler,* Revised edition (New York: Dover Publications, Inc., 1993), Section "*Review and Evaluation.*"

4. Roger Penrose, *The Emperor's New Mind* (Oxford: Oxford University Press, 1989), Ch. 6.

5. B. Greene, *The Elegant Universe: Superstrings, Hidden Dimensions, and the Quest for the Ultimate Theory,* (New York: Vintage Books), 1999, Ch. 15.

6. G. Cantor, D. Gooding and F.A.J.L. James, *Michael Faraday* (New York: Humanity Books, 1991), Ch. 3.

7. J. Wells, *The Politically Incorrect Guide to Darwinism and Intelligent Design* (Washington D.C.: Regnery Publishing, Inc. 2006), Ch. 2.

8. Michael. J. Behe, *Darwin's Black Box: The Biochemical Challenge to Evolution* (New York: Free Press, 1996).

9. J. Wells, *The Politically Incorrect Guide to Darwinism and Intelligent Design* (Washington, D.C.: Regnery Publishing, Inc., 2006), Ch. 5.

10. J. P. Moreland (Ed.), *The Creation Hypothesis,* InterVarsity Press, 1994, Introduction.

11. William A. Dembski, *Intelligent Design* (Downers Grove, IL: InterVarsity Press, 1999), Ch. 8.

Chapter 17: The Causal Creation

1. Isaac Newton, "Second Letter to Richard Bentley (1692-93)" in *The Works of Richard Bentley,* edited by Alexander Dyce (London: F. Macpherson, 1838).

2. Hugh Ross, *The Creator and the Cosmos: How the Greatest Scientific Discoveries of the Century Reveal God, Third Edition* (Colorado Springs, CO: Navpress, 2001), Ch. 14.

3. Timothy Ferris, Ed., *The World Treasury of Physics, Astronomy and Mathematics* (Boston: MA: Little Brown and Company, 1991), Section: "The Structure of the Universe."

4. Ibid.

5. Hugh Ross, *The Creator and the Cosmos: How the Greatest Scientific Discoveries of the Century Reveal God, Third Edition* (Colorado Springs, CO: Navpress, 2001), Ch. 4.

6. B. Greene, *The Fabric of the Cosmos: Space, Time, and the Texture of Reality* (New York: Vintage Books, 2005), Ch. 10.

7. B. Greene, *The Fabric of the Cosmos: Space, Time, and the Texture of Reality* (New York: Vintage Books, 2005), Ch. 7.

8. Roger Penrose, *The Emperor's New Mind* (Oxford: Oxford University Press, 1989), Ch. 7.

9. See note 7 above.

10. L. Strobel, *The Case for a Creator* (Grand Rapids, MI: Zondervan, 2004), Ch. 7.

11. J. Wells, *The Politically Incorrect Guide to Darwinism and Intelligent Design* (Washington D.C.: Regnery Publishing, Inc. 2006), Ch. 2.

12. See note 2 above.

Chapter 18: Home Sweet Home

1. Martin Rees, General Editor, *Universe: The Definitive Visual Guide* (London, UK: Dorling Kindersley Limited, 2005).

2. J. G. Luhmann, J. B. Pollack and L. Colin, *The Scientific American Book of Astronomy* (Guilford, CT: Lyons Press, 1999), Ch. III.

3. Ibid.

4. See note 1 above.

5. B. Zuckerman and M. A. Malkan, *The Origin and Evolution of the Universe* (Boston: Jones and Bartlett Publishers, 1996).

6. Ibid.

7. Ibid.

8. B. Jakosky, "Searching for Life in Our Solar System" in *The Scientific American Book of Astronomy* (Guilford, CT: Lyons Press, 1999), Ch. III.

9. Hugh Ross, *The Creator and the Cosmos: How the Greatest Scientific Discoveries of the Century Reveal God, Third Edition* (Colorado Springs, CO: Navpress, 2001), Ch. 14.

10. P. D. Ward and D. Brownlee, *Rare Earth: Why Complex Life Is Uncommon in the Universe* (New York: Copernicus/Springer-Verlag, Inc., 2000).

11. Hugh Ross, *The Creator and the Cosmos: How the Greatest Scientific Discoveries of the Century Reveal God, Third Edition* (Colorado Springs, CO: Navpress, 2001), Ch. 16.

12. M. Denton, *Nature's Destiny* (New York: The Free Press, 1998) Ch. 4.

13. Ibid.

14. See note 10 above.

15. G. Gonzalez and J. W. Richards, *The Privileged Planet* (Washington, D.C.: Regnery Publishing, Inc., 2004), Ch. 7.

Chapter 20: The Uncreative Creation

1. William A. Dembski, *Intelligent Design* (Downers Grove, IL: InterVarsity Press, 1999), Ch. 5.

2. L. Strobel, *The Case for a Creator* (Grand Rapids, MI: Zondervan, 2004), Ch. 9.

3. Ibid.

4. Access Research Network Origins and Design Archives: Interview Origins and Design 17:2, www.arn.org/docs/odesign/od172/editors172.htm.

5. C. S. Lewis, *Mere Christianity* (New York: Harper San Francisco, 2001), Ch. 4.

Chapter 21: The Stretched-Out Universe

1. F. Heeren, *Show Me God: What the Message from Space is Telling Us About God, Revised Edition, Wonders that Witness Vol. 1* (Wheeling, IL: Day Star Publications, 1998).

2. T. Ferris, *The Whole Shebang: A State-of-the-Universe Report* (New York: Simon and Schuster, 1997).

3. Ibid.

4. Hugh Ross, *The Creator and the Cosmos: How the Greatest Scientific Discoveries of the Century Reveal God, Third Edition* (Colorado Springs, CO: Navpress, 2001), Ch. 14.

5. L. M. Krauss and R. J. Scherrer, "The End of Cosmology?", *Scientific American* (March 2008): 46-53.

6. See note 2 above.

Chapter 22: The Temperature of Creation

1. E. Hecht, *Physics: Calculus* (Pacific Grove, CA: Brooks/Cole, 1996), p. 239.

2. Hugh Ross, *The Creator and the Cosmos: How the Greatest Scientific Discoveries of the Century Reveal God, Third Edition* (Colorado Springs, CO: Navpress, 2001), Ch. 4.

3. Martin Rees, General Editor, *Universe: The Definitive Visual Guide* (London, UK: Dorling Kindersley Limited, 2005).

4. Fred Heeren, *Show Me God: What the Message from Space is Telling Us About God, Revised Edition, Wonders that Witness Vol. 1* (Wheeling, IL: Day Star Publications, 1998).

5. See note 2 above.

6. See note 2 above.

7. L. M. Krauss and R. J. Scherrer, "The End of Cosmology?", *Scientific American* (March 2008): pp. 46-53.

Chapter 23: The Constants of Creation

1. D. Macaulay, *The New Way Things Work* (Boston, MA: Houghton Mifflin Company, 1998).

2. T. Ferris, *The Whole Shebang: A State-of-the-Universe Report* (New York: Simon and Schuster, 1997), Ch. 8.

3. B. Greene, *The Fabric of the Cosmos: Space, Time, and the Texture of Reality* (New York: Vintage Books, 2005), Ch. 3.

4. B. Greene, *The Fabric of the Cosmos: Space, Time, and the Texture of Reality* (New York: Vintage Books, 2005), Ch. 12.

Chapter 24: Reflections of Splendor

1. D. A. Landgrebe, *Signal Theory Methods in Multispectral Remote Sensing* (New York: Wiley-Interscience, 2003).

Chapter 25: The Waters of Creation

1. M. Denton, *Nature's Destiny* (New York: The Free Press, 1998), Ch. 2.

2. See note 1 above.

3. See note 1 above.

4. P. D. Ward and D. Brownlee, *Rare Earth: Why Complex Life Is Uncommon in the Universe* (New York: Copernicus/Springer-Verlag, Inc., 2000), Ch. 12.

5. Ibid.

Chapter 26: The Paradoxical Universe

1. Roger Penrose, *The Emperor's New Mind* (Oxford: Oxford University Press, 1989), Ch. 6.

2. Ibid.

3. B. Greene, *The Fabric of the Cosmos: Space, Time, and the Texture of Reality* (New York: Vintage Books, 2005), Ch. 4.

4. M. Kaku, *Physics of the Impossible: A Scientific Exploration into the World of Phasers, Force Fields, Teleportation, and Time Travel* (New York: Doubleday, 2008), Ch. 4.

5. See note 3 above.

6. See note 1 above.

7. See note 3 above.

8. See note 1 above.

9. See note 1 above.

Chapter 27: The Magnificent Creation

1. M. Rees, General Editor, *Universe: The Definitive Visual Guide* (London, UK: Dorling Kindersley Limited, 2005).

2. Lee Strobel, *The Case for a Creator* (Grand Rapids, MI: Zondervan, 2004), Ch. 7.

3. Hugh Ross, *The Creator and the Cosmos: How the Greatest Scientific Discoveries of the Century Reveal God, Third Edition* (Colorado Springs, CO: Navpress, 2001), Ch. 14.

4. P. D. Ward and D. Brownlee, *Rare Earth: Why Complex Life Is Uncommon in the Universe* (New York: Copernicus/Springer-Verlag, Inc. 2000), Ch. 13.

Chapter 28: His Mighty Torrential Rains

1. T. Kuhn, *The Structure of Scientific Revolutions, Revised Edition* (Chicago: The Chicago University Press, 1970).

2. J. Wells, *The Politically Incorrect Guide to Darwinism and Intelligent Design* (Washington, D.C.: Regnery Publishing, Inc., 2006), Ch. 17.

3. N. Geisler, *Systematic Theology, Volume Two, God/Creation* (Minneapolis, MN: Bethany House, 2003), App. 6.

4. Michael J. Behe, *Darwin's Black Box: The Biochemical Challenge to Evolution* (New York: Free Press, 1996).

5. W. A. Dembski, *The Design Inference: Eliminating Chance Through Small Probabilities* (Cambridge: Cambridge University Press, 1998).

6. B. Greene, *The Fabric of the Cosmos: Space, Time, and the Texture of Reality* (New York: Vintage Books, 2005), Ch. 10.

7. William A. Dembski, *Intelligent Design* (Downers Grove, IL: InterVarsity Press, 1999), Ch. 4.

8. D. D'Souza, *What's So Great About Christianity* (Washington, D.C.: Regnery Publishing, 2007), Ch. 14.

9. G. Gonzalez and J. W. Richards, *The Privileged Planet* (Washington, D.C.: Regnery Publishing, Inc., 2004), Ch. 11.

10. Hugh Ross, T*he Creator and the Cosmos: How the Greatest Scientific Discoveries of the Century Reveal God, Third Edition* (Colorado Springs, CO: Navpress, 2001), Ch. 16.

11. See note 5 above.

Chapter 29: Entropy and the Arrow of Time

1. Roger Penrose, *The Emperor's New Mind* (Oxford: Oxford University Press, 1989), Ch. 7.

2. Ibid.

3. R. Penrose, *The Road to Reality: A Complete Guide to the Laws of the Universe* (New York: Vintage Books, 2007), Ch. 27.

Chapter 31: Line Upon Line

1. J. Vacca (Ed.), *The World's 20 Greatest Unsolved Problems* (Upper Saddle River, NJ: Prentice Hall/PTR, 2005), Ch. 17.

Chapter 33: The Big Creation

1. G. Musser, "Five Essential Things To Do in Space," *Scientific American Special Report*, *Vol. 297*, The Future of Exploring Space (Oct. 2007).

2. Martin Rees, General Editor, *Universe: The Definitive Visual Guide* (London, UK: Dorling Kindersley Limited, 2005).

3. T. Ferris, *The Whole Shebang: A State-of-the-Universe Report* (New York: Simon and Schuster, 1997), Ch. 1.

Chapter 34: The Extent of the Universe

1. T. Ferris, *The Whole Shebang: A State-of-the-Universe Report* (New York: Simon and Schuster, 1997), Ch. 3.

2. Ibid.

Chapter 35: The Created Creation

1. Hugh Ross, *The Creator and the Cosmos: How the Greatest Scientific Discoveries of the Century Reveal God,*

Third Edition (Colorado Springs, CO: Navpress, 2001), Ch. 14.

2. Ligonier Ministries Radio Program.

3. Hugh Ross in *The Creation Hypothesis: Scientific Evidence for an Intelligent Designer,* edited by J. P. Moreland (Downers Grove, IL: InterVarsity Press, 1994), Ch. 4.

4. R. Penrose, *The Emperor's New Mind* (Oxford: Oxford University Press, 1989).

5. Ibid.

6. J. N. Wilford, Ed., *Cosmic Dispatches: The New York Times Reports on Astronomy and Cosmology* (New York: W. W. Norton and Company, 2001), Ch. 8.

7. B. Bickel and S. Jantz, *Creation and Evolution 101: A Guide to Science and the Bible in Plain Language*, Harvest House Publishers, Eugene, Or., 2001.

Chapter 36: The Heavens for Height

1. D. O'Shea, *The Poincare Conjecture: In Search of the Shape of the Universe* (New York: Walker and Company, 2007), Ch. 13.

2. "Cosmology's Greatest Discoveries," *Astronomy Magazine Collector's Edition* (2009).

3. Martin Rees, General Editor, *Universe: The Definitive Visual Guide* (London, UK: Dorling Kindersley Limited, 2005).

4. H. Ross, "Aliens from Another World? Getting Here from There," *Facts for Faith, Quarter 2*-2001, 24-32.

5. Martin Rees, General Editor, *Universe: The Definitive Visual Guide* (London, UK: Dorling Kindersley Limited, 2005).

Chapter 37: The Separate Creation

1. N. Geisler, *Systematic Theology, Volume Two, God/Creation* (Minneapolis, MN: Bethany House, 2003), Ch. 18.

Chapter 38: The Goodness of Creation

1. *Merriam-Webster's Collegiate Dictionary, 11th Ed.* (Springfield, MA: Merriam-Webster, Inc., 2005).

2. Ibid.

Chapter 39: The Severity of Creation

1. H. Ross, "Synchronizing Clocks in Astronomy and Anthropology with Scripture," *Reasons To Believe: Facts & Faith,* Third Quarter, Vol 10, No. 3 (1996): p. 5.

2. Lee Strobel, *The Case for a Creator* (Grand Rapids, MI: Zondervan, 2004), Ch. 7.

3. P. D. Ward and D. Brownlee, *Rare Earth: Why Complex Life Is Uncommon in the Universe* (New York: Copernicus/Springer-Verlag, Inc. 2000), Ch. 13.

4. G. Gonzalez and J. W. Richards, *The Privileged Planet* (Washington, D.C.: Regnery Publishing, Inc., 2004), Ch. 4.

5. H. Ross, *Why the Universe is the Way It Is* (Grand Rapids, MN: Baker Books, 2008), Ch. 4.

6. C. Hunter, *Darwin's God, Evolution and the Problem of Evil,* (Grand Rapids, MI: Brazos Press, 2001).

Chapter 41: The Creation Inspires

1. M. Caspar, *Kepler* (New York: Dover Publications, Inc., 1993), p. 11 of softcover version.

Chapter 42: The Secretive Creation

1. J. Macmurray, *By Chance? Landscapes from the Canvas of the Creator* (Sisters, OR: Multnomah Publishers, Inc. 1998), p. 27.

2. E. T. Bell, *Men of Mathematics*, (New York: Simon & Shuster, Inc., 2008), Ch. 6.

3. R. P. Crease and C. C. Mann, *The Second Creation* (New York: Macmillan Publishing Company, 1986), Ch. 9.

4. R. P. Crease and C. C. Mann, *The Second Creation* (New York: Macmillan Publishing Company, 1986), Ch. 2.

5. J. Jonnes, *Empires of Light: Edison, Tesla, Westinghouse, and the Race to Electrify the World,* (Random House Trade Paperbacks: New York, 2004).

6. W. A. Dembski and J. Wells, *The Design of Life: Discovering Signs of Intelligence in Biological Systems* (Dallas, TX: The Foundation for Thought and Ethics, 2008), Ch. 8.

7. F. Rana and H. Ross, *Origins of Life: Biblical and Evolutionary Models Face Off*, Navpress, Colorado Springs, Co, 2004, Ch. 8.

8. W. A. Dembski and J. Wells, *The Design of Life: Discovering Signs of Intelligence in Biological Systems* (Dallas, TX: The Foundation for Thought and Ethics, 2008), Ch. 8.

9. S. C. Meyer in *Mere Creation: Science, Faith and Intelligent Design,* (Ed.) W. A. Dembski (Downers Grove, IL: InterVarsity Press, 1998), Ch. 5, "The Explanatory Power of Design."

10. Fred Heeren, *Show Me God: What the Message from Space is Telling Us About God, Revised Edition, Wonders that Witness Vol. 1* (Wheeling, IL: Day Star Publications, 1998).

Chapter 43: The Mathematical Language of the Universe

1. Galileo Galilei, *The Assayer* (1623).

2. M. Caspar, *Kepler* (New York: Dover Publications, Inc., 1993).

3. A. R. Hall, *Isaac Newton: Adventurer in Thought* (Cambridge: Cambridge University Press, 2000), Ch. 4.

Chapter 44: To Everything a Purpose

1. Robert Dicke, "Dirac's cosmology and Mach's principle," *Nature* (1961), 192:440-441.

2. Michael Denton, *Nature's Destiny* (New York: The Free Press, 1998).

Chapter 45: The Invisible Creation

1. Isaac Newton, "Third Letter to Richard Bentley" as quoted in J. H. Brooke, *Science and Religion: Some Historical Perspectives* (Cambridge: Cambridge University Press, 1991).

2. M. Milgrom, "Does Dark Matter Really Exist?" *Science American* (August 2002): 42-52.

3. R. Penrose, *The Emperor's New Mind* (Oxford: Oxford University Press, 1989).

4. "Cosmology's Greatest Discoveries," *Astronomy Magazine Collector's Edition* (2009).

www.ingramcontent.com/pod-product-compliance
Lightning Source LLC
LaVergne TN
LVHW051823080426
835512LV00018B/2707